On Becoming Agile

On Becoming Agile

Daniel J. Power and Ciara Heavin

BUSINESS EXPERT PRESS 🔍

Leader in applied, concise business books

On Becoming Agile

Cover design by Charlene Kronstedt

Interior design by Exeter Premedia Services Private Ltd., Chennai, India

First published in 2021 by
Business Expert Press, LLC
222 East 46th Street, New York, NY 10017
www.businessexpertpress.com

ISBN-13: 978-1-63742-008-9 (paperback)
ISBN-13: 978-1-63742-009-6 (e-book)

Business Expert Press Information Systems Collection

Collection ISSN: 2156-6577 (print)
Collection ISSN: 2156-6593 (electronic)

First edition: 2021

10 9 8 7 6 5 4 3 2 1

This book is dedicated to the memory of the late
Prof. Daniel J. Power my co-author, mentor, and friend.

A Blessing (Irish version):
Go n-éirí an bóthar leat.
Go raibh an ghaoth go brách ag do chúl.
Go lonraí an ghrian go te ar d'aghaidh,
Go dtite an bháisteach go mín ar do pháirceanna
Agus, go mbuailimid le chéile arís,
Go gcoinní Dia i mbos A láimhe thú.

May the road rise to meet you.
May the wind be always at your back.
May the sunshine warm upon your face,
The rains fall soft upon your fields
And, until we meet again
May God hold you in the palm of His hand.

(Author Unknown)

Description

Becoming agile is an ongoing journey. As the global environment changes, and becomes more complex and more uncertain, the importance of increasing agility and developing an agile mindset grows. The goal of this book is to explain and facilitate the journey. We explore agile values, practices, and principles that can help people cope with volatile and ambiguous situations. Agile values improve processes and promote communication in an organization. Agile practices advance innovation through high-performance multidisciplinary teams.

Agile is about learning to anticipate and respond appropriately to the unexpected. Being agile is about interactions with people that result in successfully completing work tasks and meeting objectives. Agile is not about blindly moving faster, rather it is about continuous flexibility and learning. This book is targeted to advanced students and managers who are interested in learning to be agile. This accessible practical text poses 30 questions and provides answers that offer a starting point for further reflection.

Keywords

adaptive planning; agile; agility; agile approach; agile coach; agile development; agile leader; agile project management; agile team; agile planning; agile principles; agile organization; team lead; stakeholders; scrum; eXtreme programming; lean; kanban; feature-driven development; pareto principle; product backlog; value-driven delivery

Contents

Preface

Writing and researching *On Becoming Agile* is part of our personal journeys to become more agile. We have learned much from coaching others to be more agile. This book is neither a traditional textbook nor a memoir, but more of a retrospective summation of what we have learned. We tried to write a short, practical, readable guide to help people start an agile journey; to help revive a journey; and to help a person understand the status of their personal journey. A person's agile journey can begin and advance by reading this narrative and using the ideas to help define a personal agile vision and direction. To succeed, agile must become part of how one thinks and feels.

Our idea to author a book about becoming agile grew from a desire to help our students and others start down an agile path and begin an agile journey. Our students work on information technology (IT), information systems (IS), or business analytics projects, so we explain the basics of agile teams and agile methods in this book, but we take a broader approach and explore personal and organizational agility, as well as processes for agile teams.

Agile is not a single, monolithic framework or method, rather at best, it is a family of processes that try to deliver the values and principles of the Manifesto for Agile Software Development (agilemanifesto.org). The goal of generalizing prior agile ideas, updating, broadening, and making accessible the Manifesto values and principles has guided us. Our own successes and failures with agile have also informed our thinking. Questions like the need for a formal team leader versus emergent leadership remain unresolved.

In designing the plan for this book, we were guided by the traditional agile software development literature, especially a framework called Scrum. We consulted the Project Management Institute (www.pmi.org) Agile-Certified Practitioner curriculum along with materials from the Agile Alliance (www.agilealliance.org) and the Scrum Alliance (www.scrumalliance.org), and those sources influenced our thinking. Writings of early theorists and practitioners like Alistair Cockburn, Mike Cohn, Jim Highsmith, Ken Schwaber, and Jeff Sutherland also guided our thinking.

For the past 18 months, we have written this scholarly practitioner guide using a modified Scrum process. We tried to put what we had learned into practice to develop and refine the content. We encountered schedule and team changes, we tried novel approaches, we pivoted to meet product requirements, and we hope this final product delivers value. We were a remote, distributed authoring team during a global health crisis, so e-mail substituted for daily standups. An imperfect substitute at best. On occasion, Skype or MS Teams or Zoom were used for planning and reflection ceremonies. These calls were much better than e-mail for moving the project forward.

Our research found an increasing interest in adopting agile, but many people misunderstand or fail to understand agile and how to apply agile methods and principles. We strived to make agile concepts accessible, interesting, and understandable. *On Becoming Agile* is aimed at business students, IT/IS practitioners, and managers who have questions about agile and agility and who want to better understand and coach others. Start your journey to agile with us. Join us in an agile dance.

Acknowledgments

Many people over the years have contributed to the ideas and advice developed in this book—our students, clients for projects, readers of Decision Support News, faculty colleagues, friends in various software companies, and friends working on projects using agile methods. Also, DSSResources.com has been a vehicle to communicate our ideas and to get feedback.

Applying agile concepts has helped us draft this book as we have coped with lockdowns, remote work, increased stress, economic and social disruption. Zoom and Skype have kept us connected.

The actual production of this book is the result of the efforts of many people. Many thanks everyone at Business Expert Press (BEP) and affiliated organizations.

Last, and most importantly, we want to acknowledge the invaluable help and support of our families and loved ones. Dan thanks his wife Carol and sons Alex, Ben, and Greg. Ciara thanks her husband Finny, sons Oisin and Ronan, and her Mum and Dad.

Introduction

Digital disruption, increasing complexity, rapid change, and the resulting transformation of industries and organizations have created the need for more agile attitudes, behaviors, processes, and cultures. Coping with ambiguity, complexity, uncertainty, and volatility is challenging even with an agile mindset. Becoming more agile is important for individuals, teams, and organizations for three major reasons: (1) the requirements for faster, more responsive execution requires a reduction in bureaucratic processes; (2) changing technology environments reward more customer-focused processes; and (3) rapid collaboration and communication is now a requirement.

Organization agility refers to the ability of employees to quickly adapt to market changes and to respond rapidly and flexibly to changing needs and demands without compromising quality. Organization agility is a function of both its leaders and its members. The process of organization transformation starts with individuals becoming agile.

One way to explain agile is with a *dance* metaphor. Traditional operations and processes are often a slow bureaucratic dance, like a classic waltz. Slow dancing is an important skill to know, but most of us would not want to nor should we do that dance all the time. Today, if individuals, teams, and the broader collective organization seek to be successful, then it is necessary to perform and practice a wide variety of dances in appropriate contexts. Agile processes should have various rhythms, rituals, and styles. We all need to learn new dances, and we need to dance faster much of the time. Also, we need to be able to change dances in an elegant and seamless way. The agile dance is a medley, when the tune changes, we change dances. To do agile well, we need to learn multiple dances; to be agile, we must think and feel like a great dancer.

How do I become agile? People become agile by internalizing the agile mindset, including values and principles, and then applying the right practices and tailoring them to different situations as they arise. An agile person is committed to feedback, learning, and excellence.

Despite the heightened interest in agile, many people misunderstand or fail to understand the process of becoming agile and the need for applying agile methods and principles. For what types of projects should we use an agile process? When is a more structured approach appropriate? What is Scrum? What are the benefits and challenges of agile? What should I know about agile? These are good questions that should be explored.

Some agile approaches are appropriate for many diverse types of projects, and a mix of an agile approach coupled with a traditional approach can make organizations more agile. Some managers and organizations strive for a contingent or a *hybrid* approach—a mix of agile and more traditional processes. This discussion explores answers to broad questions and should lead to additional questions and answers. If you want to better understand being agile, read and reflect on this narrative. Our goal is to help you discover your own answers. The materials are arranged in a linear sequence, but you can read and re-read questions and answers in any sequence. Start at the beginning, start with a specific question of interest, or even start at the last question and work backward to understand the agile mindset and principles. Agile is about embracing change. Dance the multi-style agile dance and learn to do it well!

CHAPTER 1

Agile Mindset and Principles

Agile is a way of thinking and a collaborative approach used by individuals, self-organizing and cross-functional teams, and organizations. Agile assists people in evolving solutions through the division of tasks into short phases of work and frequent reassessment and adaptation of plans. Agile thinking is based upon a set of values, frameworks, principles, and tools for managing and delivering results. An agile mindset involves developing appropriate attitudes, principles, and thinking processes that support an agile work environment. Overall, being agile emphasizes adjustments, incremental delivery, collaboration, and continual learning.

This chapter explores five foundation questions, including: What are agile principles and values? What are agile ethical principles? What is agile project management (APM)? What are key agile concepts? Why is agile important? The answers to these questions establish a starting point for becoming agile.

Q1. What Are Agile Principles and Values?

Practitioners and researchers have been discussing agile processes for more than 25 years. A major conceptual advance, *The Manifesto for Agile Software Development*, was published in 2001 by 17 leaders in the field of software development. They identified four principles based upon their experiences. The manifesto states "we have come to value:

- Individuals and interactions over processes and tools
- Working software over comprehensive documentation
- Customer collaboration over contract negotiation
- Responding to change over following a plan

That is, while there is value in the items on the right, we value the items on the left more, cf., agilemanifesto.org."

An agile principle is a fundamental proposition that supports agile behavior and reasoning. The Agile Alliance (agilealliance.org) identifies 12 principles and guiding practices that support teams in implementing and executing with agility. The principles are based on the Agile Manifesto. Agile practitioners should try to understand and then internalize the following principles:

- Satisfy the customer through early and continuous delivery of valuable outputs.
- Changing requirements, even late in the project, are welcomed. Agile processes harness change for the customer's competitive advantage.
- Delivering results regularly and frequently is important.
- Stakeholders must work together daily throughout the project.
- Managers should create project teams around motivated individuals. Give them the environment and support they need and trust them to get the job done.
- The most efficient and effective method of conveying information to and within a project team is in face-to-face conversation.
- Tangible results are the primary measure of progress.
- Agile processes promote a sustainable work pace indefinitely.
- Continuous attention to technical excellence and good design enhances agility.
- Simplicity—the art of maximizing the amount of work not done—is essential.
- Outcomes emerge from self-organizing teams.
- At regular intervals, a team should reflect on how to become more effective, then adjust accordingly.

Project-Management.com identifies 10 key principles of agile software development. The project management key principles are: (1) active user involvement is imperative; (2) the team must be empowered to make decisions; (3) requirements evolve but the timescale is fixed; (4) capture requirements at a high level; (5) develop small, incremental releases and iterate; (6) focus on frequent delivery of products; (7) complete each feature before moving on to the next; (8) apply the 80/20 rule; (9) testing is integrated throughout the project lifecycle—test early and often; and (10) a collaborative and cooperative approach between all stakeholders is essential. There is some overlap of this list with the 12 Agile Alliance principles.

In brief, our summarized list of key agile attitudes and principles includes: (1) collaboration, (2) continuous improvement, (3) delivering value, (4) fact-based decision making, (5) pride in ownership, (6) respect for others and for self, and (7) a willingness to adapt and change.

There are multiple lists of agile principles, we see a commonality here. One should not memorize these principles, rather one should try to understand them, so that they guide thinking and behavior.

Q2. What Are Agile Ethical Principles?

Ethics is guided by ideas about virtue, duty, and consequences. Ethics is about who you want to *be* and how you want to act both as an individual and as part of a team. Ethical principles should guide how we behave and the decisions we make.

Agile is founded upon two statements of principles that provide ethical guidelines to agile professionals. In one of the agile processes, Scrum, five ethical values are emphasized: (1) keep commitments, (2) courage, (3) focus, (4) openness, and (5) respect. These values must be understood and *lived*. Examining these values helps internalize them; let us see what each means:

- Keep commitments—Before you make a commitment to team members, clients, and stakeholders, think carefully. A commitment obliges you to do something. If you make a promise, you have a duty to keep the promise, or explain why you cannot.
- Courage—Have the strength to take chances, to persevere in the face of obstacles, and withstand criticism and difficulties.
- Focus—Stay focused on the activity that you are trying to complete. Do not get sidetracked.

- Openness—You have a duty to be honest, do not keep secrets, and be willing to try new things.
- Respect—Consider the feelings, wishes, rights, or traditions of others. Listen. Encourage. Congratulate. Be helpful. Say thank you.

Five general ethical principles should also guide managers, professionals, and staff in agile decision making, agile processes, and agile behavior. These principles are:

- Beneficence and non-maleficence—Involves balancing the benefits of an action against the risks and costs involved and non-maleficence means avoiding causing harm. Do no harm or evil.
- Loyalty and responsibility—Always act in the best interests of the client, organization, colleagues, and society.
- Integrity—Be honest, principled, honorable, and upright; be willing to fight for one's beliefs.
- Justice and fairness—Apply a standard of rightness and fairness to judge and decide without reference to one's feelings or personal interests.
- Respect people's rights and maintain their dignity—Individuals have the right to self-determination.

These principles and values are often translated into codes of ethics and professional conduct. For example, the Project Management Institute (PMI) Code of Ethics and Professional Conduct describes the expectations practitioners have for themselves and others. The code specifies the basic obligation of honesty and fairness. It requires that practitioners demonstrate a commitment to honesty, ethical conduct, and compliance with laws and regulations. It carries the obligation to comply with organizational and professional policies and laws. The values that the global project management community define as most important are fairness, honesty, respect, and responsibility.

Ethical agile practices can reduce and even mitigate unintended consequences. The benefits of agile do not result solely from the adoption of a set of practices; rather, if agile and agility are to deliver value, then a positive system of principles and duties must also be adopted and followed, cf., Sliger (2009). To become agile, we must strive to engage in business conduct that is ethical and responsible. Also, we must act deliberately, and do what is right. In general, we must act consistently and ethically.

Q3. What Is Agile Project Management?

Applying agile values and principles when managing a project is commonly identified as Agile Project Management (APM). APM is an iterative, value-driven approach to delivering a project. Sanchez, Bonjour, Micaëlli, and Monticolo (2019) refer to this development as the *agilification* of project management.

APM is a process that involves breaking down a project into smaller, more manageable chunks to better deliver a successful project and create value. APM emphasizes methods and processes that prioritize action and feedback over planning and control (Schmitz 2018). Managing a project based upon agile principles involves continual collaboration with stakeholders and continuous improvement and iteration at every stage.

The role of a manager is to deploy, direct, and coordinate human resources, financial resources, technological resources, and other resources efficiently and effectively. Managing a project involves applying knowledge, skills, tools, and techniques to guide project activities that are intended to meet project requirements. The primary challenge of a project manager is to achieve all project goals within the given constraints. Managing most projects involves finding a balance between the three constraints of scope, cost, and time to achieve a high-quality outcome. Scope refers to what is accomplished.

APM has increased in popularity as managers try to overcome the many complex issues associated with more traditional project management approaches. In comparison to bureaucratic approaches, APM seems simple and intuitive.

According to the Project Management Institute (PMI), more than 70 percent of organizations have incorporated an agile approach, and agile projects are 28 percent more successful than traditional projects, cf., Conrad (2019). PMI (2017) reports "an actively engaged executive sponsor is the top driver of projects meeting their original goals and business intent." In the QuickStart Business Productivity Blog, Ali (2018) identifies five companies that successfully implemented agile Scrum project management, including 3M, IBM, ANZ, Google, and Spotify. IBM identified improvements in metrics such as on-time delivery, defect backlog, customer satisfaction, maintenance, and innovation, cf., Brown (2013).

APM emphasizes work organized in small chunks delivered incrementally by a collaborative, self-organizing team. Multiple teams may work on the same larger scope project. For some bureaucratic organizations and certain types of high-risk innovation projects, a pure APM approach may not be viable. A more pragmatic solution may require a balance between the stability offered by a traditional planning approach and the flexibility associated with an agile approach. Adoption of a hybrid project management approach may be an appropriate solution for high-risk projects.

Q4. What Are Key Agile Concepts?

Learning and understanding agile concepts is a starting point to becoming agile and collaborative as a project team member, team lead, coach, or manager. An agile journey requires both an understanding of concepts and practice coupled with coaching or mentoring. The words we use and how we use them is important. Agile vocabulary captures our intentions and helps us communicate effectively. Table 1.1 presents a list and explanation of six broad agile concepts.

We will further explain the brief definitions in Table 1.1 throughout the book. Agile means more than being "able to move quickly and easily" or "the ability to think and understand quickly," but those attributes are important. Agile is responsive to incomplete or changing requirements, provides short development cycles and rapid feedback, and facilitates more active customer involvement. An agile organization is a structure with decentralized decision making that is socially flat, team-oriented, and consensus-based.

The five hallmarks of an agile organization include: (1) a network of teams within (2) a people-centered culture that (3) operates in rapid learning and fast decision cycles, which are (4) enabled by technology,

Table 1.1 Key agile concepts

Key agile concepts	Description
Agile	A mindset, a way of thinking, a framework for action taking, a goal, and a journey to more contingent processes, higher performance, and potentially greater value creation.
Agility	A firm's "ability to detect opportunities for innovation and seize those competitive market opportunities by assembling requisite assets, knowledge, and relationships with speed and surprise" (Sambamurthy, et al. 2003; p. 245).
Agile development	A "time boxed, iterative approach to software delivery that builds software incrementally from the start of the project, instead of trying to deliver it all at once near the end".[1]
Agile organization	An organizing structure with decentralized decision making that is socially flat, team-oriented, and consensus-based. The five trademarks of an agile organization include: (1) a network of teams within (2) a people-centered culture that (3) operates in rapid learning and fast decision cycles, which are (4) enabled by technology, and a (5) common purpose that co-creates value for all stakeholders.
Roles	There are three essential responsibilities in any agile project: (1) product owner, (2) facilitator, Scrum Master, or team lead, and (3) team member.
Sprint	A short period of work during which an increment of product functionality is implemented.

and a (5) common purpose that co-creates value for all stakeholders (Aghina, et al. 2018). Agile organizations are enabled by self-organization, a management principle that teams autonomously organize their work. Self-organization happens within boundaries and in terms of given goals. Teams choose how best to accomplish their work, rather than receiving detailed direction from others outside the team.

A project vision statement is an ideal view of desired outcomes for the client that result from successful project completion. A project vision statement is a vivid description of the project result intended to inspire the project stakeholders to initiate the project and to guide the project team. A project vision answers the *what* and *why* questions of a project, and it provides a starting point for inspiring action.

---

[1] agilenutshell.com

These six and many other agile concepts are discussed and explained in more detail in later chapters. The glossary contains 36 important terms with definitions that should be reviewed and mastered.

Q5. Why Is Agile Important?

Agile hyperbole continues to mislead, and some see agile as a solution to every problem (cf., Ambroziewicz 2017; Mandir 2018). Agile started as an approach to software development, an alternative to the traditional software development lifecycle (SDLC) framework, and it has become much more. Agile is not a magic bullet to solve every problem, rather agile is a mindset, a way of thinking, a framework for action taking, a goal, and a journey to more contingent processes, higher performance, and potentially value creation. There are multiple agile methods, for example, Scrum, Kanban, and APM serve different purposes. Agile is a powerful concept that means an individual, team, or organization has developed capabilities of responding rapidly to change and of creating more dynamic business processes. Agile processes are especially helpful in managing the changing requirements of projects.

The Manifesto for Agile Software Development (Beck, et al. 2001) does not discard the structures and processes of prior management methods, rather agile is a way to do some tasks better and faster. An agile process is not appropriate for every project. For example, strategic decision making about irreversible alternatives should not be made using an agile process, rather the decision process should be systematic, slow, and deliberate and based upon merit, data, objective judgment, and awareness of possible consequences, cf., Ambroziewicz 2017; Bezos 2017. In many cases, however, the processes for reversible decisions should be more agile, higher velocity, and even opportunistic.

According to Rigby, Sutherland, and Takeuchi (2016), agile methodologies "involve new values, principles, practices, and benefits and are a radical alternative to command-and-control-style management— are spreading across a broad range of industries and functions and even into the C-suite." Despite the heightened interest, many people misunderstand or fail to understand becoming agile and applying agile methods and principles. In general, agile is about better communication, adapting to changing situations quickly, and rapid innovation. Agile methods are especially good at engaging and communicating with people and often result in greater involvement of stakeholders in activities and projects.

As noted previously, one way to explain agile is with a *dance* metaphor. Dance is art and science. Individuals, teams, and organizations should perform and practice a wide variety of dances in appropriate contexts. For example, agile Scrum is perhaps like a fast tango for small projects. The point is we need to learn many dance steps and styles, including tap dancing, the twist, and hip-hop if we want to be agile. A simple version of slow dancing, the two-step waltz, is often taught to elementary school students because it is much easier to learn than other more energetic dance styles. Agile processes have various rhythms, rituals, and styles. We do not want to always do the waltz.

Today, businesses need to be more agile in executing digital transformation strategies. Teams need to be more agile in software and systems development. People need to be more agile in adapting and responding to change. Agile means one can move quickly and easily and can think and understand quickly. Some synonyms for agile we like include deft, dexterous, graceful, and nimble.

The noun agility is sometimes used in business strategy, new product, and marketing discussions. Sambamurthy, et al. (2003) define agility as a firm's "ability to detect opportunities for innovation and seize those competitive market opportunities by assembling requisite assets, knowledge, and relationships with speed and surprise" (p. 245). Managers often strive to increase agility or to become more agile. One must ask if becoming agile and increasing agility is important or just another buzzword or fad of the year or decade for improving performance. Becoming more agile and increasing agility both personally and professionally are important goals for most individuals, teams, and organizations; in our opinion, agile it is *not* a passing fad.

From our perspective, business agility refers to an enterprise's ability to respond to the ongoing technology and social disruption by using processes that better meet market and customer demands. The goal of agile and agility must be to create value. McKinsey (2020) asserts "Becoming an agile organization allows a company to increase speed of execution." Agile has become much more than a set of management practices relevant to software development.

In a CIO opinion article, Ronan (2016), a retired IT Executive at Fidelity Investments, identified five reasons based upon his experiences of why organizations should be using agile. His reasons include: (1) decisions are made more quickly; (2) change is recognized as inevitable and is embraced; (3) younger employees really like the collaborative, fast-paced agile environment; (4) customer satisfaction is much higher for agile projects versus waterfall projects; and (5) agile projects had significantly fewer defects in the production environment. This list of reasons may have limited validity across organizations, but they provide arguments to test.

Becoming more agile is important for individuals, teams, and organizations for three major reasons: (1) the requirements for faster, more responsive execution require a reduction in bureaucratic processes; 2) changing technology environments reward more customer-focused processes; and (3) rapid internal collaboration and communication that is coordinated using technology is both possible and a requirement for successful individuals, teams, and organizations. Agile processes meet new needs created by digital disruption. Agility helps us change and adapt to dynamic environments.

As we noted in the introduction, we all need to learn new dances, and we need to dance faster much of the time. We need to be able to change dances in an elegant and seamless way, depending upon the need. Agile teams do not necessarily translate into business agility, rather creating strategic business agility requires agile teams for many tasks that have a customer-centric focus, cf., Almeida (2018). Becoming agile is part of a long-term strategy for digital transformation. It is important to combine changes in the business model with digital transformation to create an agile work environment. To succeed, we all need to remember that any good dancer who is dancing with a partner must dance in harmony, shared joy, and synchronicity.

Conclusion and Summary

In this introductory chapter, we have addressed a variety of related topics. Based upon our analysis, Figure 1.1 highlights six key agile principles and values, these include: (1) individual initiative and pride in ownership, (2) collaboration, (3) interaction with stakeholders, (4) self-organizing teams making fact-based decisions, (5) embracing simplicity and delivering value, and (6) continuous improvement.

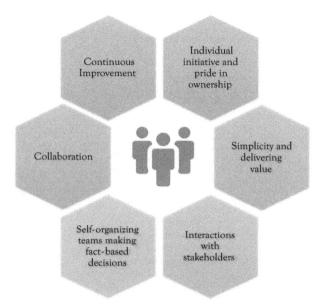

Figure 1.1 Key agile principles

In general, APM is a people-first approach where work is organized in small chunks delivered incrementally by a collaborative, self-organizing team. The values that the global project management community define as most important are fairness, honesty, respect, and responsibility. If we seek to be agile, it is our duty to be fair and honest while showing respect for others and taking responsibility for our own actions.

Agile is a mindset. To become agile, one learns a way of thinking and a framework for action taking. The goal of becoming agile and of adopting more contingent processes is higher performance and potentially greater value creation.

An agile person is responsive to incomplete or changing requirements, seeks rapid feedback, and facilitates active customer involvement. Agility is essential because there is a need for faster, more responsive processes, changing technology environments reward more customer-focused processes, and rapid collaboration and communication are required for success.

Becoming agile can be disruptive and even uncomfortable. Current practices and attitudes will change. Learning is good and knowing a mix of processes and practicing them add variety and interest. How you think about work is the most important change associated with agile and agility. Enjoy your work and do good.

CHAPTER 2

Becoming an Agile Practitioner

An agile practitioner has the experience, education, and competence to lead and direct agile projects. One can start a journey to become an agile practitioner by learning and understanding the fundamentals of agile methods. Once one has learned the fundamentals, it is important to apply the knowledge gained and to be actively engaged with applying agile principles.

As you practice agile, reflect on your experiences, and continue learning. This chapter is primarily focused on agile leadership and five questions are addressed, including: How does one become agile? What should an agile practitioner know and do? What is agile leadership? What *is* and what *is not* essential to be agile? What are the scrum framework fundamentals?

Q6. How Does One Become Agile?

Agile is not a binary concept, rather each of us, our teams, and our organizations act and behave on a continuum that descriptively ranges from awkward, brittle, bureaucratic, rigid, and fixed to graceful, nimble, lively, quick-moving, vigorous, and extremely agile as illustrated in Figure 2.1.

Agile and other related terms describe how we work with others, how we interact, and how we think about others and our world. Some of us are

Figure 2.1 Agile continuum

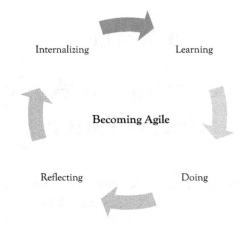

Internalizing   Learning

Becoming Agile

Reflecting   Doing

Figure 2.2 Agile cycle

extremely agile in our interactions, while others among us are slower to change and adapt, even awkward in our interactions. With software projects, agile is often more likely to result in success than more structured life cycle approaches (Chaos Report 2011). Agile is a learned state of mind and a way of thinking. To become more agile, we must learn and practice agile thinking, understand the process, and then master the process. In summary, to become agile, one should go through an ongoing cycle of learning, doing, reflecting, and internalizing (Figure 2.2).

According to Scott Ambler (2009), "agility is more of an attitude than a skillset." He cites four common characteristics of agile software developers. Those characteristics apply generally and include: "(1) open-minded and therefore willing to learn new techniques; (2) responsible and therefore willing to seek the help of the right person(s) for the task at hand; (3) willing to work closely with others; and (4) willing to work iteratively and incrementally."

Smith (2012) provides some guidance to becoming agile. He argues "Once you understand what agile really is, you need to assess how agile can help you with your business problems." He notes "Once you correlate your needs to the areas that agile helps in, you are ready to determine the level of agile you can digest effectively." It is important to use a practical approach to increasing agility to manage risk. One way to achieve this goal is by involving people from all areas of an organization to increase buy-in and ownership.

Becoming agile means that people, especially key decision makers, adopt and practice evidence-based decision making. Senior managers who seek a more agile organization must lead the way and learn to be agile and must find and use evidence in decision making. Mitchell (2019) suggests the "alternative is bleak. If they don't do so, then the illusion of control—which comes from managing circumstantial outputs—will persist until reality bites them."

Making decisions through the conscientious, explicit, and judicious use of the best available evidence from multiple sources is important. Agile decision makers ask answerable questions, acquire evidence, appraise the evidence, apply the evidence, and assess the consequences and outcomes. Agile decision makers follow a systematic process and make ethical decisions.

Becoming agile involves major change. Two approaches to understanding change seem especially relevant to completing an agile journey: (1) Lewin/Schein's change theory and (2) the Shu Ha Ri agile adoption pattern. Lewin/Schein specifies three steps: (1) unfreeze, (2) change, and (3) refreeze. Shu Ha Ri (Cockburn 2001; Fowler 2014) refers to three steps of mastery: (1) learn, (2) detach, and (3) transcend. Combining both approaches, one should take the following steps (see Figure 2.3) to become more agile:

1. Assessing, evaluating, and unfreezing: Determine how you act and respond in situations. Figure out your areas of strength and areas for improvement. Realize you can change.
2. Reading, researching, learning, and training: Learn about the Agile Manifesto and the agile philosophy, read about various methods and frameworks, watch video lectures, and attend training sessions.
3. Practicing, changing, and transitioning: Work on a variety of agile teams. Find an experienced Scrum Master (SM) or agile coach to learn from about the process and rituals.
4. Getting and giving feedback, reflecting, detaching, listening, and questioning: Feedback and reflection are an important part of learning. Feedback should be part of a continuous process of conversation, questions, and reflection. Agile implies a self-reinforcing learning and communicating cycle. At the *Ha* stage, one reflects upon and

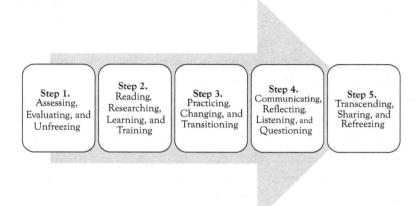

| Step 1.
Assessing,
Evaluating, and
Unfreezing | Step 2.
Reading,
Researching,
Learning, and
Training | Step 3.
Practicing,
Changing, and
Transitioning | Step 4.
Communicating,
Reflecting,
Listening, and
Questioning | Step 5.
Transcending,
Sharing, and
Refreezing |

Figure 2.3 Steps to becoming agile

    questions why agile works and when and how agile strategies are best applied.
5. Transcending, sharing, and refreezing: At the Ri stage, one strives "to keep, to detach/fall, to break away and transcend." This is a process of growth and change visualized as concentric circles of development, with Shu, traditional wisdom, within Ha, and both Shu and Ha are within or must be mastered for Ri.

Resisting change is a fundamental problem, and it is not a new problem. Despite concerns about this ongoing problem, it is wise for managers and agile coaches to be empathetic with those who see implementing agile as simply another fad or as more busy work. Engage employees, involve them, and listen to them. Communicating change effectively is our responsibility. Many people need support and understanding to cope with significant behavior and process changes.

Developing an adaptive mindset is usually challenging. A person with an adaptive or agile mindset assesses the facts and circumstances of the current situation and the environment, and then makes appropriate adjustments and adaptions required to thrive in the situation. Developing this skill and mindset requires new learning, reflection, and practice.

Becoming agile means that you know deep in your soul there is no lasting failure, only feedback. With an agile mindset, one approaches everything as a lesson, adjusting actions based upon feedback, and proceeding toward desired outcomes, and hence continually improving. An agile journey takes time and effort, but the agile destination justifies the quest to learn. One does not become agile overnight, rather one must become the change one wishes to see.

Q7. What Should an Agile Practitioner Know and Do?

Knowing agile principles and developing an agile mindset are the starting point of becoming agile. An agile practitioner should have explored, embraced, and applied agile principles in the context of a project team and organization. A person should model and demonstrate agile principles and have the knowledge to discuss agile values with others. An agile practitioner helps ensure colleagues and customers have a shared understanding of agile terminology and principles. An agile person should practice servant leadership and encourage emergent leadership within a team. One should experiment with new techniques and process ideas while contributing to a safe and trusted team environment where people experiment and make mistakes. Finally, an agile practitioner must support changes intended to make an organization more effective and efficient.

Agile practitioners and agile teams must strive to deliver valuable results by producing high-value incremental deliverables for review, early in a project and often, based on stakeholder priorities. The team should maximize the value of their work to stakeholders while minimizing non-value-added work. Stakeholders should provide feedback on these increments, and the team should use this feedback to prioritize and improve future increments. An agile practitioner should be familiar with value-based prioritization techniques like ranking, analytical hierarchy, and multi-criteria scoring. An agile team should deliver a valuable, minimally viable artifact or product to get feedback.

Engaging with stakeholders is an important activity prior to and during a project. Engaging means attempting to understand a person's needs and wants. A project team should work to create a trusting environment that aligns with the expectations of all project stakeholders. The project team should balance stakeholder requests with an understanding of the cost and effort involved and maintain transparency. The two overriding goals of stakeholder engagement are (1) to promote participation and collaboration throughout the project life cycle and (2) to provide the situational knowledge needed for effective and informed decision making.

An agile practitioner should recognize that team performance on a project depends on developing an environment of trust, learning, collaboration, and conflict resolution within the team. Such a work environment promotes team self-organization, enhances relationships among team members, and cultivates a culture of high performance. Striving for excellence must be a primary goal of an agile culture.

Borrowing from the operations management and the quality literature, agile leaders and teams should work to improve the quality, effectiveness, and value of the team product, the team processes, and perhaps, most importantly, the skills of team members. In general, organization members should strive to develop and explore agile attitudes and beliefs as part of the process of developing an agile mindset. An agile practitioner should think in terms of agile ideas and values.

Q8. What Is Agile Leadership?

Some may be skeptical about agile, and others may think the term is overused. Becoming more agile in one's behavior, in completing team tasks, and in competing with other organizations creates value and improves other outcomes. Agile training should help leaders to be more effective in complex, uncertain, and rapidly changing environments. Agile leaders are needed from the project management level to the C-suite, including the chief executive officer (CEO), chief financial officer (CFO), chief operating officer (COO), and chief information officer (CIO).

Mersino (2018) explains that there are four key things agile leaders must do, including: (1) establishing teams, (2) shaping the culture and environment, (3) coaching, and (4) leading organizational change. Senior leaders must protect and encourage agile teams. Also, senior leaders must coach agile team members to solve their own problems. An agile leader is often a servant-leader with limited *formal, coercive* power.

A team lead is an important member of a collaborative project team. With an external client, a team lead is the internal product owner for the project backlog. This person is responsible for planning, executing, and promoting the activities needed to complete a project. A team lead or project lead works with the team and key stakeholders to set goals, schedules, and major objectives. A team leader helps the team perform at its highest level. This involves removing any impediments to progress and facilitating meetings. A team leader is a coach for the team, helping the team do the best work it can. As noted, a team leader is a servant-leader, who works with and sometimes serves as the Scrum Master (SM) team self-organize, self-manage, and deliver project increments. The team, to help her team self-organize, self-manage, and deliver project increments. The team leader communicates directly with more senior managers.

A SM is one agile role in the scrum method. A person in this role may be the team lead, and a person in that role does anything possible to help team members perform at their highest level. The SM role involves removing any impediments to progress, facilitating meetings, and doing things like working with the team lead to make sure the task list or product backlog is in good shape and ready for the next short iteration or sprint.

The SM emphasizes: (1) facilitating a daily meeting or standup; (2) setting up retrospectives, sprint reviews, or sprint planning sessions; (3) shielding the team from interruptions during a sprint; (4) removing obstacles that affect the team; (5) walking the product owner or team lead through more technical user stories; and (6) encouraging collaboration between the team and client. A SM is responsible for making sure a scrum team lives by the values and practices of the scrum framework and agile. The SM is the process owner for a team. The SM role involves helping other team members communicate, coordinate, and cooperate. A SM may also directly assist in meeting project delivery goals.

As Anthony Mersino (2018) notes "Managers and Leaders are often the biggest impediment to transformation. It is an interesting conundrum— managers and leaders say they want to be more Agile, yet they are often the ones who hinder adoption or transformation." Leaders must become agile and must provide agile leadership to facilitate organization and process transformation.

An agile team leader often has limited authority usually focused solely on ensuring the team follows the agile framework process. Agile project leadership can be more difficult than serving as a typical project manager.

Project managers often have the fallback position of "do it because I say so." The times when a SM or agile team leader can say that are limited and restricted to ensuring that the scrum framework is being followed.[1]

Q9. What *Is* and what *Is Not* Essential to Be Agile?

We who are involved in the culture of agile processes and agility are bombarded by buzzwords, technical jargon, and colorful metaphors. We must sort out what is essential for increased agility and what concepts are dated, jargon, and overly colorful metaphors. Ideally, agile must be widely understood in an organization to change a culture and help employees and teams become more agile. Agile knowledge cannot be the esoteric realm of the few, owned and understood by only a small number of people with specialized knowledge or deep interest.

Today, managers need an easy-to-understand set of agile ideas with limited use of jargon. Agile should be implemented in accord with agile principles within an organization and its culture. The multiple agile frameworks and methodologies share similar philosophies, characteristics, and practices. Implementation of each agile approach means understanding competing practices, terminology, and tactics. Managers need to know what is essential and what is not; our assessment is presented in Table 2.1.

In Table 2.1, what is deemed essential cannot be forgotten or ignored. Those tasks that are listed as not essential are applied and adopted at the discretion of the team, members, and organization leaders. Do not become overly concerned with the formality of agile approaches and methods. The key to becoming and being agile is one's personal resiliency and thought processes.

Q10. What Are the Agile Scrum Framework Fundamentals?

Answering this question summarizes the concepts and practices associated with the widely used agile scrum approach. Scrum is an agile framework and structured set of ideas that is intended to help teams collaborate on

---

[1] cf. https://mountaingoatsoftware.com

Table 2.1 Assessment of agile tasks

Essential/Not Essential tasks	Explanation
Essential: Know agile principles and hold agile values	We value our colleagues and our interactions with colleagues and stakeholders; we collaborate openly and honestly with stakeholders; we want to deliver results frequently, and in meaningful increments; and finally, we anticipate change in our plans, and we embrace and respond to change as we implement our plans.
Essential: Have a *daily* task-focused project team meeting	The meeting keeps an agile team focused on results. Asking structured questions about progress and plans is crucial, calling the meeting a daily scrum is not. Standing during the meeting is a good practice and calling the meeting a daily *standup* reminds us to stay focused on high-quality task completion.
Essential: Have a plan, prioritize tasks, keep track of progress, and revise tasks to reflect new needs and changes	Start with a *To-Do* list, pick high-priority tasks to try to accomplish in each work period. Add tasks, revise tasks, even delete them as seems appropriate. Think from your customer's point of view when defining tasks. Tasks should be focused and big enough to track and small enough to complete in a reasonably short time period.
Essential: Reflect, think about what was done	Consider what worked well and what could have been done better following a defined, short work period, often 2 weeks. How much was accomplished?
Essential: Find ways to create and increase value for customers and stakeholders	Know how they define value. Measure what is finished.
Not essential: The ritual of agile approaches.	We can choose to use or ignore jargon like time-boxed and colorful metaphors like scrum or eXtreme Programming (XP).
Not essential: To always use an agile approach.	It is not necessary to use an agile approach for every project and activity. Simple projects that are highly structured can be completed quickly with a traditional structured project approach.
Not essential: There is no need to obsess on terms like product versus project, or product backlog and sprint backlog	A backlog is a *To-Do* list, there is nothing magical. Use a term only if it helps your understanding or the understanding of others. User stories are not appropriate or needed for every project. There are many acceptable ways to define and specify tasks. A team accomplishes work and delivers value.
Not essential: Do not obsess about creating agile artifacts	Such as burndown charts, story points, and preparing calculations for the amount of work completed in a sprint, the so-called velocity of project completion. Measure what is finished.
Not essential: Encouraging more hype about agile	There is no need for exaggerated statements or claims. It is better that adopting agile exceeds expectations.

complex tasks. Scrum.org materials states "Scrum is a framework within which people can address complex adaptive problems, while productively and creatively delivering products of the highest possible value. Scrum itself is a simple framework for effective team collaboration on complex products." Also, scrum (short for scrummage) is a method of restarting play in rugby football that involves players packing closely together with their heads down and attempting to gain possession of the ball.

Scrum has gained popularity over the years because of its simplicity and its capability to incorporate various overarching practices in other agile models. Much has been written about scrum, and this discussion abstracts and interprets three primary sources—the Schwaber and Sutherland (2017) *Scrum Guide*, Rubin's (2013) *Essential Scrum*, and Nicolas's (2018) *Scrum for Teams*.

Ken Schwaber and Jeff Sutherland (2017), two authorities on scrum, assert that

> Scrum's roles, events, artifacts, and rules are immutable and although implementing only parts of Scrum is possible, the result is not Scrum. Scrum exists only in its entirety and functions well as a container for other techniques, methodologies, and practices.

Their view is an absolutist starting point for learning about scrum. The path to agility requires active learning and participating in project teams that use scrum. This discussion attempts to complement and summarize the official scrum framework, cf., Schwaber and Sutherland (2017).

Scrum is a lightweight, easy-to-understand framework and process. Lightweight means that scrum has only a few rules and practices, and they are easy to follow. The more one studies scrum and learns about the framework, the more complexity that is encountered. Mastering scrum is a challenging, ongoing quest. Scrum is a framework for guiding a process, it is not a methodology or a step-by-step recipe. The scrum framework identifies what needs to be done, and the scrum team must figure out how to do it. Scrum must be interpreted and modified to fit a specific situation and set of circumstances. All scrum elements or parts are needed to create an effective process and to deliver a valued result. The three pillars of scrum are (1) transparency, (2) inspection, and (3) adaptation. The pillars emphasize transparency of the significant aspects of the process, an inspection of progress to goals, and adaptation and adjustment as needed to minimize problems.

The scrum framework consists of scrum teams and their associated roles, events, artifacts, and rules. Each component within the framework serves a specific purpose and "is essential to Scrum's success and usage." The rules of scrum bind together the roles, events, and artifacts, governing the relationships and interaction between them. The essence of scrum is a small team of people. A scrum team is highly flexible and adaptive.

In Q1, we refer to the five scrum values of commitment, courage, focus, openness, and respect that must be understood and *lived* by the scrum team. These principles and values create a code of behavior for a team member that must be understood and followed. Examining the definitions for these values helps internalize the values. By pursuing these values, the three scrum pillars of transparency, inspection, and adaptation gain meaning and can help build trust for everyone. Scrum team members learn and explore these values as they work with the scrum events, roles, and artifacts.

Schwaber and Sutherland (2017) claim "Successful use of Scrum depends on people becoming more proficient in living five values." First, people must personally commit to achieving the goals of the scrum team. The scrum team members must have the courage to do the right thing and work on tough problems. Everyone on the team must focus on the work of the sprint and the goals of the scrum team. The team and its stakeholders must agree to be open about all the work and the challenges with performing the work. Finally, scrum team members must respect each other.

Success with scrum also involves learning seven fundamentals including (1) the roles and responsibilities, (2) learning to write requirements and user stories, (3) creating and managing the product or project backlog of work, (4) estimating effort and prioritizing backlog items, (5) planning and executing a short duration sprint, (6) conducting sprint reviews and retrospectives, and (7) appreciating the *Definition of Done* and why it is important to know when a project is *Done*.

Scrum team roles include a product owner, the development team, and a Scrum Master (SM). Scrum teams are described as self-organizing because members choose how best to accomplish tasks and create value. Teams consist of people from different areas of an organization who have diverse skills that are needed for a specific, complex project. The product owner is a single person who is responsible for managing the product or project backlog, the list of features, changes, tasks, or other activities that when completed, achieve specific outcomes. The development team is the professionals who do the work and deliver "a potentially releasable increment of 'Done' product at the end of each Sprint." The SM is a servant-leader for the scrum team who helps everyone understand scrum theory, practices, rules, and values.

A daily scrum meeting is a 15-minute time-boxed meeting held early in each workday where each development team member answers three questions: (1) What have you done since the last scrum meeting? (i.e., yesterday), (2) what will you do before the next scrum meeting? (i.e., today), and (3) What prevents you from performing your work as efficiently as possible? Another way to express the questions is to ask: (1) What tasks have you worked on since we last talked? (2) What tasks are you planning to work on next? (3) Is anything getting in the way of finishing the work as expected? The SM must ensure participant discussions do not go too far outside these constraints. The scrum literature recommends that this meeting take place first thing in the morning as soon as all team members arrive.

Product backlog (*project backlog* or *backlog*) is the list of requirements for a system, expressed as a prioritized list of product backlog items. These include both functional and non-functional customer requirements, as well as technical team-generated requirements. While there are multiple inputs to the product backlog, it is the sole responsibility of the product owner to prioritize the product backlog.

The SM is a facilitator for the team and product owner. Rather than manage the team, the SM works to assist both the team and product owner in the following ways: (1) remove the barriers between the development team and the product owner so that the product owner directly drives development, (2) teach the product owner how to maximize return on investment (ROI) and meet his or her objectives through scrum, (3) improve the lives of the development team by facilitating creativity and empowerment, (4) improve the productivity of the development team in any way possible, (5) improve practices and tools so that each increment of functionality is potentially shippable, and (6) keep information about the team's progress up to date and visible to all parties, cf., Schwaber (2004).

A sprint is an iteration of work during which an increment of product functionality is implemented. In general, an iteration should not last longer than 30 days. The sprint starts with a one-day sprint planning meeting. Many daily scrum meetings occur during the sprint (one per day). At the end of the sprint, we have a sprint review meeting, followed by a sprint retrospective meeting. During the sprint, the team must not be interrupted with additional requests. Guaranteeing the team will not be interrupted allows it to make real commitments it can be expected to keep.

The sprint backlog defines the work for a sprint. It is the set of tasks that must be completed to realize the sprint's goal(s) and selected set of product backlog items.

A sprint goal is the result of a negotiation between the product owner and the development team. Meaningful goals are specific and measurable. Instead of "Improve scalability," try "Handle five times as many users as version 0.8." Scrum focuses on goals that result in a demonstrable product. The product owner is entitled to expect the demonstrable product (however small) starting with the very first sprint. In iterative development, subsequent sprints can increase the robustness or size of the feature set.

A sprint planning meeting is a negotiation between the team and the product owner about what the team will do during the next sprint. The product owner and all team members agree on a set of sprint goals, which is used to determine which product backlog items to commit from the uncommitted backlog to the sprint. Often, new backlog items are defined during the meeting. This portion of the sprint planning meeting is time-boxed to four hours.

A sprint retrospective meeting is held at the end of every sprint after the sprint review meeting. The team and SM meet to discuss what went well and what to improve in the next sprint. The product owner does not attend this meeting. The sprint retrospective should be time-boxed to three hours.

A stakeholder is a person or a group or organization external to the scrum team with a specific interest in and knowledge of a product that is required for incremental discovery. It is represented by the product owner and actively engaged with the scrum team at a sprint review.

User stories are one of the primary development artifacts for scrum and XP project teams. A user story is a very high-level definition of a requirement, containing just enough information so that the developers can produce a reasonable estimate of the effort to implement it. A user story is a unit of work that should be completed in one sprint. Smaller than that is a task. A user story helps to create a simplified description of a requirement. In agile scrum, a user story is a description of the objective, which helps a person to achieve a feature.[2]

The Official Scrum Guide by Schwaber and Sutherland (2017) summarizes the fundamentals. The framework has few rules, but problems do arise. Common problems include: (1) too much reliance on scrum software tools that often hinder team and client interactions; (2) lack of a full-time SM and lack of training and experience of the SM; (3) lack of a single, designated product owner; (4) poor team collaboration spaces; (5) poor coordination with other project teams and with a project management office (PMO); and (6) lack of organizational commitment to agile and scrum processes and principles, cf., Eljay-Adobe (2018); Rubin (2013).

Conclusion and Summary

Agile is a learned state of mind and a way of thinking. To become an agile practitioner, one must learn and practice agile thinking, understand, and then master the process. Agile practitioners and agile teams must strive to deliver value by producing incremental deliverables for early review based on stakeholder priorities. An agile practitioner should recognize that team performance depends upon developing an environment of trust, learning, collaboration and communication, and conflict resolution. Agile leaders and teams should work to improve quality and, perhaps, most importantly, the skills of team members.

A team lead works with the team and key stakeholders to set goals, schedules, and major objectives. An SM is a role in the agile scrum method that provides leadership. An agile team leader often has limited coercive authority.

---

[2] https://romanpichler.com/blog/10-tips-writing-good-user-stories/

The popular agile scrum framework identifies what needs to be done, and then, the team must figure out how to do it. This approach is common to all agile processes. Agile processes must be interpreted and modified to fit a specific situation and set of circumstances. All elements or parts of the process are needed to deliver a valued result.

To become agile, one must: (1) know agile principles and hold agile values; (2) have a *daily* task-focused team meeting; (3) have a plan, prioritize tasks, keep track of progress, and revise tasks to reflect new needs and changes; (4) reflect and think about what was done well and what could have been done better; and (5) find new ways to create and increase value for customers and stakeholders.

In summary, to become an agile practitioner, one should go through an ongoing cycle of learning, doing, reflecting, and internalizing.

CHAPTER 3

Agile Approaches and Value-Driven Project Delivery

In this rapidly changing world, leaders and managers must respond better to stakeholder needs by focusing on and delivering *value*. Value is defined by a project or an organization's stakeholders, especially clients and customers. Agile leaders and teams should focus on solving problems and delivering value, rather than upon simply following a plan.

There are many agile approaches that have similarities and important differences. Part of becoming agile involves developing an understanding of what approach or framework fits a specific situation. There is no universally accepted agile method that is appropriate for all circumstances and situations.

This chapter examines five questions: What is value-driven delivery of projects and work? What are various agile approaches? What is solution-focused agile? What is an agile framework for projects? How can we measure the value and success of agile?

Q11. What Is Value-Driven Delivery of Projects and Work?

Project managers, team leads, and other managers are encouraged to make project decisions that result in value. *Value* may refer to monetary gain, to new capabilities, or to any valuable outcomes. Customers and stakeholders ultimately assess value. Many people place great importance and higher value on what they can see and touch. For example, decision support software is evaluated based upon the user interface that people can see and manipulate. Software is a tangible aspect of project work, as opposed to the intangible benefits of greater productivity in some projects. Value is a measure of both tangible and intangible benefits created through the delivery of goods or services. Value is usually more than financial benefits and value is often estimated, projected, or forecasted prior to starting a project.

According to Oswald (2016), "value-driven delivery is a combination of value-adding and risk-reducing activities." A project that increases customer satisfaction will also deliver value to an organization. Components of value must be commensurable, meaning components must be measurable by the same standard so that comparisons can be made.

Tangible value can be measured and is concrete. The tangible value of a work product represents the benefits that are quantifiable and measurable. Intangible value results from a belief that the system will provide important, though hard-to-measure benefits to the customer, company, or organization.

Value-driven means that value is the major decision criterion in prioritizing project deliverables, requirements, and user stories. The highest-value items are delivered first whenever possible. Constraints may alter the priorities but delivering value should be first and foremost on the minds of team members.

Managers, stakeholders, and the project team must forecast or project cost, schedule, budget, resource requirements, technology trends, and project value. Forecasting the value of a project and its components helps managers decide whether a project is beneficial and should proceed or if it is better to stop the project. Each task and user story has a value that is based upon potential benefits and potential costs of delivering it. A project has the highest value when its value exceeds that of alternative uses of the resources. Some projects have a short payback period to regain the net amount invested.

The product owner and team members should routinely reassess the value of items in the product backlog and prioritize the items, requirements or tasks, and user stories based on value to the client or customer. Backlog items can be added, removed, reprioritized, and redefined. In some situations, backlog items are classified in one of the three categories as (1) meeting basic needs, (2) meeting performance needs, or (3) meeting excitement needs. Generally, those items classified as meeting basic needs have higher value and higher priority. The items that are put in a specific sprint backlog should generally be the high-value items remaining in the project or product backlog.

Delivering value to the customer is crucial. The customer is paying for the final deliverable, whether a product or service. Customers assess value both before and after delivery of the product or service. Know your customer and what the customer values. Collaborate with the customer to better understand what is valued. Business owners want a return on their investment as well.

Q12. What Are the Various Agile Approaches?

Practitioners have been refining and trying various agile approaches for more than 25 years. Originally focused on completing software development projects, agile is now viewed as a way of approaching tasks and work. Specific approaches may deliver more value than another in each situation. There are many agile approaches, including Scrum, Kanban, Lean, eXtreme Programming (XP), Crystal, Dynamic Systems Development Method (DSDM), Feature-Driven Development (FDD), and Test-Driven Development (TDD). Learning about multiple frameworks will increase versatility and help you participate in a wide variety of projects. The most popular agile approach is Scrum. Table 3.1 presents an overview of the five major agile approaches, Scrum, XP, Kanban, Lean, and FDD.

Scrum is the most widely followed agile framework worldwide, but it is not always the best for a specific project. Choosing the most appropriate approach depends upon the objectives of the project, the resources available (including staff and time constraints), and the stakeholders involved. These approaches share the same philosophy, as well as many of the same characteristics and practices. Each of these promotes stakeholder engagement, with the aim of delivering the right product to the right customer at the right time. Agile is an umbrella term that includes multiple project management approaches.

Q13. What Is Solution-Focused Agile?

It is important to examine the past to learn from our mistakes, but we need to also examine *what will work* to deliver results in each situation. Solution-focused agile is a mashup of techniques from multiple disciplines that promote using reflection to encourage innovation and a *what works is good*

Table 3.1 Major agile approaches

Agile approach	Description
Scrum	A lightweight agile project management framework that can be used to manage iterative and incremental projects. Scrum projects by their nature typically involve knowledge-intensive work. Scrum clearly defines key roles in the project, which promote task transparency and task ownership for the duration of the project life cycle. Scrum has gained increasing popularity over the years because of its simplicity, proven productivity and performance gains, and ability to incorporate various overarching practices promoted by other agile approaches.
Extreme Programming (XP)	XP is widely used for coding-intensive software development projects. Teams generally pick one or possibly combine two agile approaches. XP aims to produce higher-quality software and a better quality of life for the development team. XP is the most specific of the agile frameworks regarding appropriate engineering practices. XP is intended to improve software quality and responsiveness to changing customer requirements by promoting simplicity in software development design, development, maintenance, and revision.
Kanban	Kanban is about visualizing your work, limiting work in progress, and maximizing efficiency. Both Scrum and Kanban are frameworks that help teams adhere to agile principles. An agile team uses Kanban boards to continuously improve the flow of work. At its core, Kanban is concerned with incremental process improvements.
Lean	Lean is an approach for creating more value for customers with fewer resources. Lean agile follows agile principles using fewer resources. Managers in a lean organization understand the importance of delivering customer value, and they focus on continuous improvement of key processes.[1] Lean is a concept that is used with other terms such as lean product development, or lean software development.
Feature-Driven Development (FDD)	FDD is a client-centric, architecture-centric, and pragmatic software process. It is an iterative and incremental software development process. It uses any processes and practices that promote a client-valued functionality perspective. FDD emphasizes walkthrough of domains, as well as design, code, and inspection.

enough attitude. Holding agile retrospective meetings are a good addition to any work environment, but adding a more prospective, future-oriented component helps teams to improve processes, handle controversial issues, and focus attention on solutions to barriers and problems.

---

[1] https://lean.org/WhatsLean/

Enterprise Agile Coach Maurice Hagar (2019) explains that

Ninety-two percent of executives say agility is critical for the future of their business, yet only 4% of their transformation efforts are delivering agility. The leading causes for this gap are an entrenched legacy culture and general resistance to change.

Delivering business agility requires organization wide cultural change. Hagar (2019) asserts that managers are discovering that a *solution focus* is the missing piece for transforming the culture.

Finding solutions and delivering results is important. Leaders, managers, and teams encounter problems and must find a means of solving a specific problem or dealing with a demanding situation. Problems do not usually disappear, rather actions must be taken to remedy and resolve a problem. In some situations, doing nothing may resolve a problem, but evidence should suggest that doing nothing is the best path.

Some intractable problems do exist that are difficult and seemingly impossible to solve. These problems benefit from *reframing*. Framing refers to how one structures or presents a problem or an issue. Framing involves explaining and describing the context of the problem in an understandable manner. Stakeholders are the key to reframing or restating a problem. What is the problem? Who identified the problem? When and why? A well-stated problem is easier to solve than a poorly stated one, and framing should reflect the attitudes and beliefs of stakeholders. A key to innovation and creativity is the framing of problems (Getzels 1975; Getzels and Csikszentmihalyi 1976).

Problem finding is also important. A problem cannot be solved or resolved until it is adequately and appropriately identified. Problem finding is a thinking process in which a person articulates or states a barrier or issue that should be addressed, a question that needs to be answered, or a solution that is not working.

Doing agile should not narrowly focus on following a specific framework, practice, or technique. Being agile means that one broadly emphasizes agile principles and values, attitudes, and agile behaviors, cf., Abtin 2018. Solution-focused agile means the team uses an agile framework, but the focus is on solving problems in the context of agile values, see Figure 3.1. As discussed in Chapter 1, the guiding principles of agility

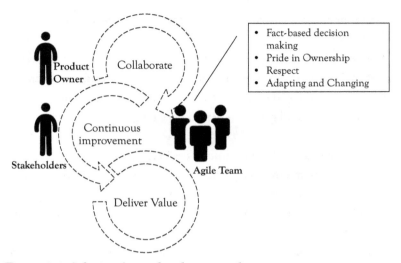

Figure 3.1 Solution-focused agile approach

include: (1) collaboration, (2) continuous improvement, (3) delivering value, (4) fact-based decision making, (5) pride in ownership, (6) respect for others and for self, and (7) a willingness to adapt and change.

In general, reason and facts rather than passion should guide agile processes. Passion and emotion may influence ethical judgments, but in business situations, decisions and project goals are generally made to meet customer needs and create value for stakeholders. Fear of failure may positively impact choosing a solution that best meets relevant decision goals and leads to project success, but a solution-focused agile process is much better than relying on fear to achieve positive outcomes.

Q14. What Is an Agile Framework for Projects?

An agile framework or methodology guides teams in an iterative and incremental delivery of a project goal and delivery of a defined *product*. A modern agile framework supports the entire life cycle of a project, from initiation to close. An agile framework is a broad guide to taking action.

Using an agile framework is especially appropriate for tasks that benefit from collaboration. Smaller scope, discrete projects related to software development, business analytics, decision support, and digital transformation are especially suited to agile development. Large-scale enterprise projects benefit from creating discrete tasks completed by agile teams. Project-oriented organizations benefit from an agile culture. According to McGannon (2013), "Agile project management … is an excellent choice for teams that work in product development, programming, business analysis, and other collaborative areas. But it's a fragile process that requires the right scope, goals, and management."

Using an agile framework assumes team members understand agile. Also, attitudes and culture must support an agile working environment. As we have noted, people should encourage mutual respect, collaboration, continuous improvement, and must have the ability to adapt to change. Teamwork starts with respecting teammates. Overall, the purpose of using agile project management is to respond to changes and additions to a project quickly.

Highsmith (2004) prescribes his Agile Project Management (APM) framework as a series of steps that take a project from an initial vision to the final delivery of an outcome or *product*. The ordered phases of the APM framework are: (1) envision, (2) speculate, (3) explore, (4) adapt, and (5) close. Table 3.2 briefly explores each of these phases.

In our opinion, agile is the guiding project philosophy and the Scrum Framework, Crystal, XP, etc. are the specific rules and directions used day to day by a team.

Ken Schwaber and Jeff Sutherland (2017) developed and explain Scrum. They state that

> Scrum's roles, artifacts, events, and rules are immutable and although implementing only parts of Scrum is possible, the result is not Scrum. Scrum exists only in its entirety and functions well as a container for other techniques, methodologies, and practices.

Schwaber and others refer to agile and Scrum as frameworks and not methodologies because the word methodology seems too prescriptive. Scrum provides a structure for delivery but does not tell you how to do specific practices. Agile encourages and promotes continuous, incremental improvement to reach the desired outcome. Modern organizations need both an agile framework for work and rigorous project management.

Table 3.2 Overview of the APM framework

Phase	Phase description
1. Envision phase	The initial phase of project management within an APM framework. In general, after approval of a business case, the agile key members are involved in the envision phase where they collaborate to create a compelling vision for a project. This phase identifies a client's or customer's vision of the project, decides the key capabilities required in the project, sets the business objectives of the project, identifies the quality objectives of the project, and identifies the right participants and stakeholders of the project and plans how the team will deliver the project.
2. Speculate phase	The product vision is translated into a backlog of requirements. In this phase, the overall approach to meet the requirements is planned and a high-level release plan for the product is presented. Two key activities occur: (1) The team must come up with at least an initial understanding of the requirements for the project. Each feature will be further broken down into one or more *user stories* for the team to discuss and estimate. The requirements also must be prioritized so that the team knows in what order to start working on them. (2) The second task is to determine a high-level milestone-based plan based upon how long it would take to create those features. This planning happens at multiple levels such as release level, wave level, and iteration level.
3. Explore phase	Agile team members explore various alternatives to implement and fulfill the requirements of a project. In this phase, work deliveries and testing take place. Here, the product vision needs to be transformed to a release plan and then to the respective iteration plan. The team works in an iterative manner in the explore phase, which means they take a sub-set of the product's features or stories and accept them into a plan for an iteration. Then, the team will proceed to work on the development of the stories. This phase goes hand-in-hand with the adapt phase, where the team learns from the experiences during development and the feedback from the customer. This is the phase where you produce the product.
4. Adapt phase	The agile team reviews the results of execution, the current situation, performance of the team against the plan, and adapts as per the requirements. Adaptation can be changing the approach to a project, changing the process, changing the environment, changing the project's objectives, and so on, to meet the requirements of the customer or client. Taking feedback, acknowledging it, and adapting to the situation based on the feedback are the major work tasks in this phase.
5. Close phase	Close is the process of finalizing all activities. For example, providing final deliverables to the client or customer, delivering documentation, archiving project materials, releasing staff and equipment for other projects, and informing stakeholders of the completion of the project. This phase concludes a project in an ordered manner capturing the project's key lessons or lessons learned.

Q15. How Can We Measure the Value and Success of Agile?

Agile is a complex, abstract concept, and there is no single way that individuals and teams *do* agile. Both factors make it challenging to identify and measure the value and success of agile in general. The Annual State of Agile reports provide insights into the application of agile across different areas of the enterprise. The surveys show increasing adoption of agile, but there remains disagreement about measuring agile success. It is not easy to measure the agile process; however, it is not an option to use these concerns as excuses for not measuring value and success. Rather, managers should identify a group of key performance indicators (KPIs) and periodically check the usefulness of the metrics.

To show progress as part of the agile journey, we must assess whether we are living up to the agile principles and delivering value as part of a project. The adage "what gets measured gets done" is important in agile organizations and for agile projects. Assessing value and success can and should be done at an individual, team, and organizational level. Both quantitative and qualitative approaches may be used to measure project goals. These approaches could include individual employee 360° reviews, individual and team surveys, post-implementation evaluations, and eliciting feedback from a variety of stakeholders including other teams and customers.

There are a variety of frameworks and approaches for measuring the success of agile, both on a day-to-day basis and overall, for agile initiatives. Four overarching metrics can be used to facilitate and track agile success; see Figure 3.2.

Productivity: This measure may include: (1) reduction in waste—how is duplication of work and handoffs reduced or even removed; (2) increased efficiency—how much work is done per unit time. For example, how many user stories or features have been designed and developed as a measure of how much the team is delivering; (3) continuous improvement—how well work is flowing through the agile development life cycle, identifying tangible measures of process improvement; and (4) on-time delivery—measuring if the agreed upon high priority backlog items (tasks) are delivered on time.

Predictability: This criterion is linked directly to the productivity of the team or organization. Agile teams measure the Planned-To-Done

Figure 3.2 Measuring agile success

ratio of a project using the product backlog items, to establish what percentage of items are complete in a specific time period and how much can be achieved during the time remaining in the project. This allows the team to measure the extent to which work is completed at a sustainable pace on average. Ask, are we meeting expectations?

Satisfaction: This may be measured in terms of (1) client satisfaction with outputs, and (2) quality. Quality may be measured using both quantitative and qualitative approaches. Product or service quality is measured by conducting a technical assessment of the product or service using a variety of DevOps models and tools. Customer satisfaction may be assessed through surveys and interviews with customers and other project stakeholders. Ask, are we creating value, and if so for whom?

Stability: This factor measures the *health* or stability of the team (employees), and it impacts productivity, satisfaction, and predictability. If organization members are motivated, collaborative, and share a common goal, the more stable and sustainable are the other measures over time.

There is no single measure or group of measures that must or should be used to evaluate agility and a specific agile project. Depending on the team, the project, and the stakeholders, different measures may be identified to objectively establish the success and value of an agile project and strategy.

Overall, if we are to understand and highlight the impact of becoming agile, there must be a balance between measuring value and success and its impacts on individual communication, performance, and productivity. We do not want to negatively impact individuals or teams. The suggested metrics should not be used to micromanage individuals or teams, but rather to shine a light on good practice and to help agile teams build on lessons learned from one project to the next. We must assess the assertion that when agile is scaled across an organization, everyone experiences the benefits. We must regularly measure the value and success of agile.

Conclusion and Summary

Value is a measure of the benefits created through the delivery of goods or services as part of an agile project. Delivering value to the customer is crucial. Customers determine value both before and after delivery of the product or service. As a general rule, it is important to collaborate with the customer to better understand what they value.

Practitioners have been trying various agile approaches including Scrum, Kanban, Lean, Extreme Programming (XP), Crystal, Dynamic Systems Development Method (DSDM), Feature-Driven Development (FDD), and Test-Driven Development (TDD). To become agile, it is important to learn about multiple frameworks. This knowledge will increase your versatility and help you participate in a wide variety of projects.

Solution-focused agile reconciles multiple techniques from various disciplines that promote using reflection to encourage innovation and a *what works* approach. Both retrospective meetings and a more prospective, future-oriented approach help people improve outcomes. Becoming solution-focused involves employing techniques such as problem finding and framing to overcome challenges that are seemingly difficult to solve.

There are many well-known, widely used agile frameworks that provide a structure for delivery, but do not tell you how to do specific practices. Agile projects still require rigorous project management.

Our analysis, experiences, and review reinforce our conclusion that there is no single measure or group of measures that must be used to evaluate agility. We identified four key indicators that can be used to facilitate and track agile value and success. These include: (1) productivity, (2) predictability, (3) satisfaction, and (4) stability. These metrics should be used to highlight good agile practices and help agile teams deliver value to customers. We should measure and reflect upon what worked and what needs improvement. Also, we must regularly ask how much value is enough to satisfy stakeholders.

CHAPTER 4

Collaborative Leadership, Stakeholder Engagement, and Performance

In agile organizations, future-oriented, collaborative leaders are important to achieving outstanding performance. Providing supervision, monitoring group performance, and developing an organization structure are important traditional skills to cultivate. Modern leaders need to especially focus on coaching, task performance, and producing results. Also, modern leaders must empower others and provide feedback to develop and motivate them.

Both client and stakeholder engagement are important determinants of success. For this reason, it is necessary that a project leader encourages and facilitates discussions between stakeholders and the project team. A team should make sure that stakeholders know what to expect regarding features, schedule, and cost.

Agile is generally more responsive than traditional hierarchical approaches to evolving user demands, inputs, and needs. Agile teams must interact with and influence project stakeholders to maximize overall benefits.

This chapter examines five questions: When is an agile approach most appropriate? How do collaboration tools support agile teams? What determines team performance on a project? What is stakeholder engagement? What should stakeholders expect in an agile environment?

Q16. When Is an Agile Approach Most Appropriate?

In general, agile is most appropriate when project requirements are uncertain, stakeholders seek rapid results, change is likely, requirements are ambiguous, and a project is complex. Agility is a means of coping with a complex, uncertain, volatile environment, where facts are ambiguous and disputed. Bureaucratic, rigidly plan-driven organizations and project teams are generally more efficient in stable, mechanistic environments. In some circumstances, a hybrid approach can combine agile and planned, bureaucratic approaches in the same organization.

A frequent choice facing managers deals with two questions: (1) how to organize and (2) what process to use to complete a project or task. Frequently, decision makers use criteria or factors to choose among alternatives related to these questions. Many factors should be considered, including: (1) requirements; (2) size and scope; (3) flexibility of the design; (4) planning and control; (5) the stakeholder; (6) developers' knowledge, skills, and experiences; (7) need to alter existing software; and (8) risks known and their potential impact.

Scrum expert, Mike Cohn, of Mountain Goat Software asserts

the most appropriate projects for agile are ones with aggressive deadlines, a high degree of complexity, and a high degree of novelty (uniqueness) to them. We want to use agile when we are doing something that is new . . . And in today's world, there is almost always a sense of urgency.

Mike has been building high-performing software development teams and organizations for many years.

In a thoughtful blog post, Jose Santana (2016) discusses six indicators that agile is the most appropriate project management method. He argues first and foremost use agile when project requirements are uncertain; second, when project teams are co-located and can benefit from daily Scrums; third, when there is a proactive product owner because real-time feedback is key for success in agile; fourth, when teamwork and collaboration are important and teammates are likely to show initiative; fifth, when there is a willingness to fail and learn fast; and sixth, when management supports use of the agile framework and its culture of empowering teams. Remote teams are increasingly successful in using agile.

In her blog post entitled *Agile vs. Waterfall: Matching Method to Project Requirements* (2018), Eileen O'Loughlin argues "you need to be proficient at both agile and waterfall PM practices so you can apply the right methodology, to the appropriate projects to achieve the best results." Neither agile nor waterfall is always the best, and managers should not use one approach exclusively. Eileen identifies four factors that make agile a better fit than a waterfall approach. These factors include situations with: (1) unclear requirements, (2) a high level of participation and buy-in from stakeholders, (3) the cost of change is minimal, and (4) there is an emphasis on teamwork and continuous improvement.

Many authors seem to favor a hybrid or contingency approach to implementing agile with a more plan-driven approach that creates well-defined deliverables at the beginning of a project. Agile managers must have experience with multiple approaches for managing and completing a project. A manager should be more a coach and decision maker than a taskmaster or a specialist on a team. If your primary stakeholder wants lots of upfront planning, approvals at each stage of a project or task, extensive documentation, and your culture is formal and structured, then stick with bureaucratic, highly structured processes. In general, agile processes will fail in such a situation. Processes must be designed, managed, and controlled.

Q17. How Do Collaboration Tools Support Agile Teams?

Agile philosophy emphasizes collaboration and communication among team members and with clients and other stakeholders. A wide variety of computer-based software supports people who are working together on common projects across time zones, long distances, and at various physical locations. A collaboration tool can be as simple as an e-mail and as complex as multiuser project management software applications. Managers must understand the benefits and limitations of collaboration tools and should be familiar with software available to support teams. This discussion is an overview, and it suggests guidelines for choosing the right tool(s) for a specific project.

The purpose of a collaboration tool is to help a group of two or more people accomplish a common goal. Bika's (2019) short article provides brief descriptions of four communication tools and 10 collaborative project management tools. Some tools are very narrow and specific in their capabilities, while others are more general. The four communications tools Bika thought especially relevant include (1) Flowdock chat support, (2) GoToMeeting videoconferencing, (3) Slack instant messaging and file transfer, and (4) WebEx personalized video meeting rooms.

Nieuwland (2017) evaluates Workzone and then examines competing products or services. His review emphasizes the broad category of project management collaboration tools. Table 4.1 presents collaboration tools that seem especially useful for agile work environment.

Table 4.1 Collaboration tools for agile work

Collaboration tool	Description
Asana (https://asana.com)	Helps plan, organize, and manage projects for small teams. Users may assign tasks to other members, add followers to projects, and monitor deadlines.
Google's collaboration tools include Google Docs and Sheets	These tools allow teams to edit files at the same time and save all the changes automatically.
monday.com (https://monday.com)	A tool that simplifies the way teams work together. Users can manage workload, track projects, move work forward, and communicate with people. Previously known as Dapulse, it "has a great visual design so it's easy to understand and work with."
MS Teams (https://microsoft.com/en-ie/microsoft-365/microsoft-teams/group-chat-software)	A business communication platform offered as part of the Microsoft 365 suite of applications. MS Teams offers workspace chat and videoconferencing, file storage, and MS application integration.
Redbooth (https://redbooth.com/)	Formerly Teambox, a cloud-based project management, collaboration, and communication platform. Its platform allows users to plan and collaborate through many functions from videoconferencing to creating Gantt charts.
Skype (https://skype.com/en/)	Another Microsoft tool, a telecommunications application that specializes in providing video chat and voice calls between computers, tablets, mobile devices, and supports instant messaging.
Trello (https://trello.com)	Includes features such as boards, lists, and cards that enable you to organize and prioritize your projects. It is easy to learn and works well for monitoring projects and assigning tasks. Trello also makes using agile, Scrum, and other project management frameworks easy.
Workzone (https://workzone.com)	Project management tool, users can view status updates with cross-project dashboards.
Zoom (https://zoom.us/)	A widely used video-enabled communication too. It is easy to use and allows remote teams to communicate and collaborate.

The well-known general-purpose tools used in collaboration and communication, including Zoom, MS Teams, and Skype, are widely available. Choosing a tool can be challenging because many possibilities are available. Start at product websites. Check the product features and costs. If a free demonstration version is available, try it. Pick a tool that is easy to learn, intuitive to use, and easy to maintain. Small teams need different tools than large, distributed teams. Pay for only the features you need. Evaluation criteria should include: (1) user interface (UI), (2) ease of use, (3) integration capabilities, (4) value-added, and (5) features and functionality. In general, a cloud-based tool will be the best choice.

Computer-based tools are fast becoming the primary way that people collaborate and communicate. These tools can help teams manage and organize projects. A computer-based tool can centralize daily tasks and provide team members with a means to view status.

Q18. What Determines Team Performance on a Project?

A project team is a group of people assigned to work on a project. Team member attitudes and abilities, skills, team processes, tools, and team leadership determine team performance. Also, the project environment can hinder or support project success. Overall, team performance on a project depends upon developing an environment of trust, learning, collaboration, and conflict resolution within the team and with stakeholders. Such a work environment promotes team self-organization, enhances relationships among team members, and cultivates a culture of high performance. Performance is better when the primary goal of the team is striving for excellence.

Research suggests that the more a team develops as a cohesive group, learns together, and collaborates, the better the performance of the team. Motivated, competent teams have better performance than mediocre, demotivated teams. Leaders should strive to develop the competencies of team members and ensure the most competent people have the most influence on a team's actions and decisions.

A collaborative leader seeks out a diversity of opinions and ideas among teammates to build strategies and solve problems. Collaborative leaders are important to team performance. Teams that have worked together on other projects have developed behaviors and relationships that influence performance in both good and bad ways. One should consider prior experiences and successes of people when assembling and creating project teams. Successful teams are *highly cohesive*, members are committed to each other and the project. On a committed team, the members strive for excellence. Effective communication within a team is crucial to developing a high-performing team. A stable, manageable group of skilled people is also important to team success. Experience suggests a team committed to self-organizing process management and agile principles also contributes to project excellence and success.

A study of teams at Cisco found there are three key areas that distinguish the best teams: (1) teammates perform tasks that play to their strengths, (2) high-performing teams have high levels of trust and safety, and (3) team members share a sense of "how they can win together," cf., Hammett (2019). Research participants in the study of Cisco teams (Bradley, et al. 2013) expressed the opinion that the collective intelligence and diverse perspectives of people working together creates better overall results.

According to a study by Pentland (2012), the ideal team player circulates "actively, engaging people in short, high-energy conversations. They are democratic with their time—communicating with everyone equally and making sure all team members get a chance to contribute. They're not necessarily extroverts, although they feel comfortable approaching other people. They listen as much as or more than they talk and are usually very engaged with whomever they're listening to. We call it 'energized but focused listening.' The best team players also connect their teammates with one another and spread ideas around. And they are appropriately exploratory, seeking ideas from outside the group but not at the expense of group engagement."

Hansen (2016) asserts "adopting an agile methodology allows your team to quickly adapt when project plans change instead of panic. It also forces your team to communicate constantly and focus on quality over quantity." Becoming agile will improve team performance on a project.

Teams must collaboratively make trade-offs. Evaluating priorities while dealing with constraints is known as the trade-off space. The four key variables that can be adjusted are: (1) time, (2) project scope, (3) cost or expenses, and (4) quality. All four of these are interdependent; changing one variable has implications for others. It is important to recognize that there are natural trade-offs among them. For example, if you want faster completion, then you will need to do less, or use more resources, or produce a lower-quality product. If you want to spend exactly X dollars, then the team will have to work a specified number of hours, perhaps do less work, or change the quality of the project output. Teams make choices with stakeholders that determine project outcomes.

In summary, Figure 4.1 illustrates the important factors determining team performance, which include: (1) a cohesive, committed team; (2) collaboration and communication; (3) adequate resources; (4) the team composition, structure, and processes; (5) team stability; (6) a manageable team size; and (7) effective collaborative leadership. External, less controllable factors also influence team performance, including a reward system, training or technical assistance, and the organizational culture, cf., Harris (2010).

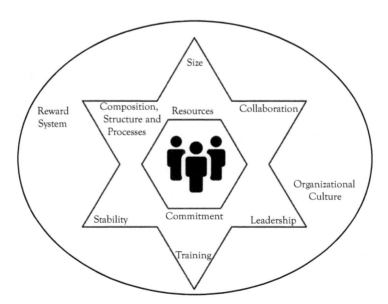

Figure 4.1 Team performance determinants

Q19. What Is Stakeholder Engagement?

Stakeholder engagement and stakeholder management are the most important ingredients for successful project delivery. Stakeholder engagement is a process used to involve people who may be affected by a decision so that they may influence the choice and implementation of the decision.

The AccountAbility 1000 Stakeholder Engagement Standard defines stakeholders as

> ... those groups who affect and/or could be affected by an organization's activities, products or services and associated performance. This definition does not include all those who may have knowledge of or views about the organization. Organizations and projects may have many stakeholders, each with distinct types and levels of involvement, and often with diverse and sometimes conflicting interests and concerns.

Stakeholder engagement is generally defined as the process used by an organization to engage *relevant* stakeholders for a purpose to achieve agreed-upon outcomes.

Stakeholder management implements actions and strategies to meet stakeholder needs and interests, and the process attempts to ensure effective implementation of communication plans, engagement actions, and strategies.

The role of the stakeholder varies depending on the project methodology. Scrum methodology for software development projects takes a narrow view of the role of stakeholders. Scrum prescribes three well-defined stakeholder roles: product owner, Scrum Master, and development team. The product owner is responsible for understanding what other interested parties want and for summarizing their views. More traditional project management methodologies and certifications, such as Project Management Professional (PMP) certification or PRojects IN Controlled Environments (PRINCE2), define stakeholders as anyone impacted or affected by a project. This broad view means stakeholders can include the development team, product owner, project manager, customers, and other employees. Stakeholders want to understand what progress an agile team has made.

Organizations must remain relevant to survive in a challenging business environment and to be relevant requires that managers and teams have regular interaction and collaboration with stakeholders. Effective engagement helps translate stakeholder needs into organizational goals and creates successful outcomes. Discovering consensus about shared motivations helps a group of stakeholders to arrive at a decision and helps ensures a meaningful outcome.

Q20. What Should Stakeholders Expect in an Agile Environment?

In an organization environment, both internal and external stakeholders have and develop expectations when interacting with, engaging, or participating in an agile process or project. As more teams, departments, and organizations endeavor to be more agile, it is important for managers and other stakeholders to anticipate and shape expectations about what is most likely to happen.

Stakeholders typically affect or are affected by an agile process or project in some way. All stakeholders should not have the same expectations, but there should be some similar ones. During a project, all stakeholders are not directly involved in creating the product, but they may participate or contribute to the process in many ways at different intervals. Some stakeholders provide technical expertise, while others contribute to decisions about which features are important. An agile project evolves through continuous improvement cycles of development, inspection, and adaptation.

Stakeholders have different duties and authority when participating in a project. Roles may change as a project proceeds. A stakeholder role may range from occasional contributions to full project sponsorship. The product owner will expect ongoing involvement. This goes beyond articulating the requirements and returning at the end of the project to inspect the results. Product owners should expect to be heavily engaged throughout. Product users should expect to provide feedback in a structured way during the project. Other stakeholders may include employees in the organization who may provide input at key stages depending on the focus of the project. Stakeholders should expect little change in requirements to maintain stability during project sprint activities.

Stakeholders have different stakes and vary in influence and attention to and interest in a project. Stakeholders with high power and a high level of interest should be consulted regularly. Other stakeholders should be kept informed as appropriate and high-power and low-interest stakeholders should be kept satisfied, cf., Mitchell, et al. (1997); Usmani (2019).

For an agile approach to succeed, stakeholders should participate actively during an agile process. This engagement needs to be planned, communicated, and revised during the interaction. It is important that members of an agile team know the relevant stakeholders, their interests, and what stake they have in the project. Agile projects benefit when stakeholders understand agile values, principles, and practices. Stakeholders should expect uncertainty, and they should expect the project team will manage uncertainty through short, time-boxed iterations, anticipation of impediments, and adaptation and rapid response to create value.

Managing stakeholder expectations around their engagement with a project is integral to success. Often, stakeholders have diverse or conflicting objectives, these differences need to be articulated and resolved if possible. Expectations can make or break the delivery of successful outcomes in an agile work environment. Stakeholders should expect to be actively involved in providing information, knowledge, and opinions.

Conclusion and Summary

Agile is most appropriate in a situation where requirements are ambiguous and uncertain, change is likely, stakeholders want fast results, and the project is complex. Agile is less appropriate for projects with a broad scope that require a large resource commitment.

Collaboration and communication are essential to the success of agile projects. Computer-based tools help teams manage and organize projects. A computer-based tool can centralize daily tasks and provide team members with a means to view status. Computer-based tools facilitate both remote and face-to-face engagement.

There are seven important factors that determine team performance, including: (1) adequate resources; (2) a cohesive committed team; (3) regular collaboration and communication; (4) effective leadership; (5) a manageable team size; (6) the team composition, structure, and processes; and (7) team stability. Agile teams have an evolving structure, are usually small, with 7–9 members, and they have a diverse, heterogeneous composition.

Stakeholder engagement is a process used to involve people who may be affected by a decision. Stakeholders typically affect or are affected by processes and projects in some way. Managing stakeholder expectations is integral to success, but often, stakeholders have diverse or conflicting objectives. Any differences in expectations among stakeholders need to be articulated and resolved as quickly as possible.

Performance and delivering value have always been important, but now stakeholders want valuable results faster. Evidence suggests that using agile with collaborative leaders can better meet stakeholder expectations.

CHAPTER 5

Understanding Agile Planning

Agile does involve planning, even though it is adaptive and incremental. Some may observe agile processes and view them as unplanned and even chaotic. This negative perception is usually far from the truth. It is true that agile plans are evolving and responding to requests for changes.

In an agile environment, typically, the most complex and challenging tasks are worked on first. At any time, task priorities may change and shift. In an agile environment, teams create a work backlog, which is a prioritized task list. Short, simple descriptions called user stories are the most common approach to expressing user needs.

Agile planning has a distinct rhythm that some refer to as phases or steps. Most agile projects adopt some method or approach that is defined and understood by participants. To become agile, one must understand agile planning. It is not comprehensive and bureaucratic, rather it is systematic and responsive to team, situation, and stakeholder needs.

Let us explore five key questions: How can managers overcome complexity? What is adaptive planning? What is Project Portfolio Management (PPM)? Do agile processes have phases or steps? What are the INVEST criteria for evaluating project tasks?

Q21. How Can Managers Overcome Complexity?

Managers are often working in complex environments with rapid change. This situation is unavoidable, and it is increasingly common. As part of the job, a manager must learn about their environment to successfully act, adapt, and understand. However, complexity itself poses several challenges to managerial learning, including misinterpretation of situations, the ambiguity of feedback and information, and a lack of accurate data.

The solution to working in more complex environments is to be better prepared and to strive to be a professional manager.

Many management roles are specialized, management tasks are often complex, and projects have expanded in scope and complexity. Examples of management practice areas where complexity is increasing rapidly include building, managing, and operating of information technology (IT) systems, managing continuous processing systems, and managing diverse assets. In simple management situations, time and tasks can be managed intuitively by a competent person, but complex projects require a more analytical approach.

Peter Drucker's book (1954), *The Practice of Management*, examined management as a whole and recognized that a manager had identifiable and separate responsibilities. Drucker identified a need to examine management practices. His ideas promoted recognition of management as a professional discipline. Some would disagree that management is a *profession*, but the need for more well-prepared *professional* managers has increased in modern, complex organizations.

Drucker emphasized the need for clarity about the meaning and purpose of a business. He argued that the questions "what is our business" and "what should it be?" are the most important questions a successful manager has to address. Answering those two questions has become more challenging because of increased complexity. In formulating corporate strategy, answering these questions is important for business analysis and for the formulation of mission statements. Managers must also ask "who are our customers?" and "what is the business trying to do for its customers?"

According to Drucker (1954), "The manager is the dynamic, life-giving element in every business" who defines the organization's mission, develops, and retains productive teams, coordinates various activities, sets goals, and gets things done. The tasks remain the same, but because of increasing complexity, performing them competently requires more knowledge and skill.

From Drucker's perspective, management entails farsighted thinking about the future state of things and taking appropriate risks to capitalize on opportunities. Additionally, he felt "managing a business must be a creative rather than adaptive task. The more a management creates economic conditions or changes them rather than passively adapts to them, the more it manages the business" (p. 73).

According to Drucker, managers promote the dominant cultural norms and values in the organization through their actions. These values are evident in the decisions a manager makes concerning who to recruit, who to retain and promote, the goals that are pursued, and the ethical parameters used to frame and assess decisions. Managers face more ethical questions, and cultural norms are often in transition or in dispute.

The practice of management in large organizations has become more complex, but tools, especially computer-based tools, have been developed to augment or assist managers in such environments. Tools include software for project management, tools for improved communication, and tools to retrieve information and help analyze data. Assisted or augmented decision making is needed, and managers should become more adept in their use and more agile in their own behavior.

Management remains a rational activity *tested by performance alone*. New tools help extend managerial abilities to rationally cope with complex environments and complex organizations. Management remains an emerging profession, and professional management is increasingly needed to cope with complexity. Managers in many organizations require a mastery of a complex set of accumulated knowledge and skills developed through formal education with appropriate qualifications and certifications.

Q22. What Is Adaptive Planning?

Adaptive planning is a process and theory for coping with change and complexity. Adaptive planning ideas have been applied and discussed in multiple disciplines. Agile planning is one form of adaptive planning. In an agile environment, planning occurs frequently in project teams and at broader organization levels. Rolling waves of planning occur as a project or task progresses and as details become clearer. Activities and tasks are time-boxed and completed in discreet chunks. Managers assess task complexity and estimate task effort. Adaptive planning is a human process that can perhaps be imitated or assisted using software-based decision and planning support. Adaptive planning is the ability to plan forward but altering the plan as circumstances change.

Alterman (1988) defines adaptive planning as "an approach to planning in the commonsense domain." An adaptive planner takes advantage of the characteristics of a planning situation by basing its activities on a memory of existing plans.

Adaptive planning is a useful skill in an agile environment. Agile teams should produce and maintain an evolving plan, from initiation to closure, based upon goals, values, risks, constraints, stakeholder feedback, and a review of outcomes. Adaptive planning is agile planning and timeboxing.

Planning occurs at multiple levels within an organization. At the strategic, long-term planning level, both forecast-driven and adaptive, iterative planning is useful. At the project management level, some formal, structured planning is required to determine project teams, overall project goals, and broad resource allocations. During a project, the project team should generally use adaptive planning.

Adaptive planning is an iterative process for organizing information flows, analyses, and special studies, facts, and opinions into decisions.

There are four general stages commonly associated with adaptive planning. Figure 5.1 illustrates these, including: (1) situation assessment—the analysis of internal and environmental factors that influence business performance, combined with a comparison of past performance relative to objectives and expectations; (2) strategic thinking—identification of

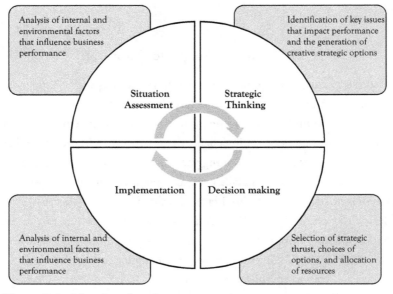

Figure 5.1 Adaptive planning process

key issues that have a major impact on performance and the generation of creative strategic options for dealing with each issue; (3) decision making—the selection of strategic thrust, choices of options, and allocation of resources in light of mutually acceptable objectives; and (4) implementation—ongoing activities that translate strategic decisions into specific programs, projects, and near-term functional action plans. The process is iterative because the implementation phase will eventually be followed by a revised situation assessment, cf., AMA Dictionary.

Adaptive planning should begin with an overriding objective or vision statement that defines the purpose and value of the activity, new product, project, or initiative. Although agile projects are not solely *plan-driven*, planning is an important activity, and projects must be planned at multiple levels, including the strategic and iteration level. In adaptive, rolling wave planning (the progressive elaboration method), the plan evolves as the project progresses. The plan is continuously modified, detailed, and improved as newer and improved information becomes available to the project management team.

> In this method, projects are kicked off with limited available information, which is used to create a high-level plan and estimates. As details emerge later in the project, plans and estimates are constantly revised to ensure they remain valid and current, cf., PMI ACP.

Agile planning identifies chunks of work performed for a finite period. This is often called timeboxing, setting a fixed time limit for an activity or backlog item. A key principle is that the fixed time limit cannot be exceeded. Activities that are scheduled in a timebox but are not completed, or in some cases, started, are rescheduled to a later planning period. A timebox can be set for any duration, but generally, all timeboxes of a project are of the same duration.

Predictive planning for traditional plan-driven projects and strategies is sometimes appropriate, but freezing goals and requirements for an entire project or a long-planning horizon is increasingly challenging and inappropriate. Computerized decision support and analytics can assist with adaptive planning.

In both routine and novel situations, people must adapt and seek facts. Planning and thinking often help people adapt prior responses to new uses or purposes. Adaptive planning attempts to explain and describe how we adapt and how we can improve our actions. Adaptive planning increases predictability in an agile environment.

Q23. What Is Project Portfolio Management?

PPM is a coordination and control process that selects, prioritizes, and staffs programs and projects to align them with organizational strategies. Programs focus on achieving goals and benefits aligned with organizational objectives. Programs are comprised of a collection of projects focused on achieving more specific goals and requirements related to an overall program. Many organizations have multiple internally and externally focused projects that require coordination. A project portfolio is an organized grouping of programs and related projects.

PPM is the centralized management of one or more project portfolios. PPM is a means to achieve strategic objectives, coordinate implementation, and improve project selection. PPM can promote agility and help create value. There is some evidence that PPM minimizes project risks, maximizes resource utilization, helps routinize agile processes, and leads to more coordinated decision making (Bridges 2018).

When managers identify a group of related projects and then define them as a program, there is a perceived need to coordinate the projects to realize synergistic benefits. Programs include the specification of the projects and the management effort and infrastructure needed for the program. Defining a program often includes tasks related to managing the program itself.

Internally focused projects and programs deliver benefits to an organization by enhancing current capabilities or by developing new capabilities. Some projects within a program can deliver useful incremental benefits to the organization before the program itself has been completed. PPM is useful for managing both analytics and decision support projects.

Program management is the centralized coordinated management of a specific program to achieve the program's benefits and objectives. PPM involves aligning multiple projects to achieve program goals and allow for optimized or integrated cost, schedule, and effort. Projects within a program are related through a common outcome or a collective capability that is delivered. If the relationship among the projects is only that of a shared client, seller, technology, or resources, the effort should be managed as a portfolio of projects rather than as a program. In programs, it is important to identify, monitor, and control the interdependencies among the components. Program and portfolio management focuses on project interdependencies and help to determine the best approach for managing them.

During a program's life cycle, projects are initiated, and the program manager oversees and provides direction and guidance to the project managers. Program managers coordinate efforts between projects but do not manage them. Essential program management responsibilities include the identification, monitoring, and control of the interdependencies between projects; dealing with the escalated issues among the projects that comprise the program; and tracking the contribution of each project and the non-project work to the consolidated program benefits.

The Agile Project Management (APM) framework is a modern agile framework that covers the entire life cycle of a project. The APM framework was proposed by Jim Highsmith (2010) in his book, *Agile Project Management*—creating innovative products.

Highsmith defines the APM framework as a series of steps that take a project from an initial vision of a product to the final delivery of the product. As we discussed in Chapter 3, there are five discrete steps or phases in the APM framework. The ordered phases of the APM framework are (1) envision, (2) speculate, (3) explore, (4) adapt, and (5) close. In general, after approval of a business case, the agile key members are involved in the envision phase where they collaborate to create the compelling vision for a project. In the speculate phase, the product vision is translated into requirements. In the explore phase, agile team members explore alternatives to fulfill the requirements of a project. This phase occurs iteratively during sprints. In the adapt or retrospective phase, an agile team reviews the results of execution, the current situation, performance of the team against the plan, and adapts as per the requirements. Finally, the close phase occurs following the last sprint and concludes the project in an ordered manner capturing the project's key lessons.

An organization's strategy should be linked with the tactical project and program execution to enhance performance and maximize returns.

Aligning projects with strategy is important. Managers should measure changes and improvements across the entire organization in terms of efficiency, predictability, and control that results from managing project portfolios. You can only manage what you measure but measuring alone is not enough (Peppers 2018). One cannot know if a project is successful unless success is defined and tracked. Identify project goals and then define how to measure and evaluate project success.

Q24. Do Agile Processes Have Phases or Steps?

Some methods classified as agile do refer to and define phases or steps. The *phases* in agile processes are overlapping and some are iterative. Many developers learned the Systems Development Life Cycle (SDLC) phases, and some find it convenient to use that terminology. There are several agile SDLC models. For example, Scrum primarily emphasizes the construction life cycle. A broader view begins with the (1) concept phase and pre-project planning, (2) inception or warm-up and project initiation, (3) construction iterations, (4) transition to the *end game*, and finally, (5) production and possibly (6) retirement (Ambler 2009). A wide range of activities overlap in these cycles or phases.

Agile processes are organized in a manner that fits the project and team perceptions and needs. Recall, agile is an iterative approach where a team delivers work in small, but meaningful, increments. So, an agile process must support incremental deliverables.

As discussed in the previous question on PPM, agile projects are often managed in five stages, called the agile life cycle. According to Highsmith (2004) and Parziale (2017), the APM framework is a series of steps that take a project from an initial vision of a product to the final delivery of the product. These phases, steps, or stages are not discrete, and overlap can occur in iterations.

Briefly, the steps have related purposes. During the envision phase, the team and stakeholders determine the desired outcomes. The speculate phase is where team members develop a dynamic backlog of the workload. Then, team members explore various alternatives. The adapt and review phase is when results are evaluated. The close phase is when the client signs off and the team has a broad retrospective on what was learned that can be applied to future engagements.

There are two key activities in the speculate phase:

1. The team must produce at least an initial understanding of the requirements. Each feature will be further broken down into one or more *user stories* for the team to discuss and estimate. The requirements also must be prioritized so that the team knows in what order to start working on them.

2. The second task is to determine a high-level milestone-based plan. So, phases or steps can be part of agile processes, but agile coaches, project managers, and other leaders in an organization need to figure out what approach and steps work best for each organization. A manufacturing organization may produce better results with one method, a retail chain may want a modified agile project approach like Scrum, and a pharmaceutical company may implement a more traditional phased approach with iterations. Different environments and circumstances require various approaches.

Q25. What Are the INVEST Criteria for Evaluating Project Tasks?

As noted in prior responses, evaluating project tasks is challenging. One approach uses the acronym INVEST (Wake 2000). INVEST stands for *I*ndependent (of all others), *N*egotiable, *V*aluable, *E*stimable, *S*mall (to fit within an iteration), and *T*estable (in principle, even if there is not a test for it yet). The INVEST criteria help one to remember a widely accepted checklist to assess project tasks and user stories. If a task fails to meet one of the criteria, the team may want to reword or rewrite it.

In 2004, the INVEST acronym was among the techniques recommended in Mike Cohn's book *User Stories Applied: For Agile Software Development*. Cohn argued "The best way to build software that meets user needs is to begin with 'user stories': simple, clear, brief descriptions of functionality that will be valuable to real users."

Evaluating a project makes sure it is on course for creating value. A team lead or manager should monitor and evaluate project tasks using criteria like INVEST before and during the project. The primary criterion used to evaluate proposed and completed projects should be the value generated for the enterprise, society, and stakeholders. Projects have intended outcomes, results, and features that are perceived by decision makers and stakeholders. Also, these outcomes should be assessed and evaluated prior to investing in and starting a project.

Once a project is completed or good enough, then it is important to determine if goals and objectives were met to help stakeholders decide if the project produced planned results, delivered expected benefits, delivered value, and resulted in the desired change.

Conclusion and Summary

Agile planning is a means managers can use to overcome complexity and uncertainty. Agile is adaptive and incremental. Agile planning is evolving and responding to requests for changes that better deliver value. Management roles are increasingly specialized, management tasks are often complex, and projects have expanded in scope and complexity. Management remains a rational activity *tested by performance alone.* New tools help extend managerial abilities to rationally cope with complex environments and complex organizations.

Adaptive planning is a process and theory for coping with change and complexity. In an agile environment, planning occurs frequently in project teams and at broader organization levels. Adaptive planning should be an iterative process of organized information flows, analyses, and special studies, to gather facts and opinions and then reach decisions. There are four general stages commonly associated with this evidence-based process, including: (1) situation assessment, (2) strategic thinking, (3) decision making, and (4) implementation.

Recall, in Table 3.2, we offer a more detailed explanation of the five phases in the APM framework: (1) envision, (2) speculate, (3) explore, (4) adapt, and (5) close. Agile organizations require agile planning processes. Senior managers must design, revise, and use processes that adapt to the changing environment of an organization.

CHAPTER 6

Finding Success: Detecting Roadblocks and Resolving Issues

Being agile means working in a highly responsive way. Agile methods have only a few rules and practices, or only ones that are easy to follow. If you have become agile, you are delivering products and services that a customer wants when they need them.

In completing an agile project, a major part of the agile leader's job is to manage and help resolve roadblocks identified by the team. To resolve problems, it is important to examine them from diverse points of view. Detecting problems and resolving them involves asking the right questions to understand the situation.

Agile leaders must understand what is important, and they must coach others in agile thinking and approaches. An experienced agile leader can influence the success of a project. Experience helps cope with adversity and roadblocks. There are many challenges to becoming agile, but persistence, practice, and patience are the key to becoming agile.

This chapter examines five questions: What is the Pareto Principle? What is the role of an agile coach? How do experience and self-discipline impact agility? How does an agile person cope with adversity? What are common barriers and challenges to becoming agile?

Q26. What Is the Pareto Principle?

Becoming agile means a person, a group, and an organization as a whole understands and applies the Pareto Principle. In 1906, Vilfredo Pareto, an Italian economist, observed a pattern for many events and situations. The Pareto Principle states that, in many situations, roughly 80 percent of the effects come from 20 percent of the causes. This principle is also sometimes stated as 80 percent of results are because of 20 percent of the effort. The Pareto Principle is also called the 80–20 rule or the principle of least effort. In decision making, project management, operations, and action taking in general, we must try to determine what the crucial 20 percent is in a situation.

In his *Forbes* article, Kruse (2016) provides diverse examples that illustrate the 80/20 rule:

- 20 percent of the sales reps generate 80 percent of total sales.
- 20 percent of the most reported software bugs cause 80 percent of software crashes.
- 20 percent of patients account for 80 percent of health care spending.

Mullaiselvan (2009) asserts

Pareto's Principle, the 80/20 Rule, should serve as a daily reminder to focus 80 percent of your time and energy on the 20 percent of your work that is important. Do not just "work smart," work smart on the right things.

Remember that in general, 20 percent of your efforts yield 80 percent of the desired results. Fried and Hansson (2010) advocate for a satisficing approach to work effort and expected outcomes. They argue "When good enough gets the job done, go for it."

The Pareto Principle has some empirical support, but for managers, the value comes from understanding that all tasks do not deliver equal value. Prioritizing tasks based upon the anticipated contribution to project and organization success helps ensure that resources are used most appropriately. Managers must figure out what tasks are most important.

The Pareto Principle is a heuristic guide to making decisions and allocating resources. Roughly 80 percent of the output from a given situation or system is determined by 20 percent of the input. Pareto analysis is a decision-making technique that uses data to find out what is most important. To use Pareto analysis, identify and list problems and their causes. Dam (2019) at the Interaction Design Foundation proposes two key questions that may help identify opportunities and address frustrations and resolve issues arising from work effort:

- Which 20 percent of your current efforts are resulting in 80 percent of your desired outcomes and happiness?
- Which 20 percent of your current efforts are causing 80 percent of your problems and unhappiness?

A Pareto chart analyzes the frequency of problems or causes in a process. It is a bar chart depicting measurements in categories. Common measures include frequency, quantity, cost, and time. After ranking the data bars in descending order, a line graph is used to depict the cumulative percentage of the total number of occurrences, total costs, or total time. For example, in manufacturing, a Pareto chart can be used to show the relative frequency of defects. The chart provides evidence for identifying improvement activities. Another example from operations, categorizing and charting customer complaints can help identify the most important problems to correct. A Pareto chart is a prioritization tool.

Some consider that the Pareto Principle is a principle in agile management and even the most important principle. It is similar to the principle stated "Simplicity—the art of maximizing the amount of work not done—is essential." Understanding that it is important to "work smart on the right things" is a key to agility.

Overall, Pareto analysis helps managers prioritize and determine what has the greatest influence on overall goals. The 80–20 rule can be applied to any area of business, including IT, design, sales, and HR (Dam 2019). Prioritization helps minimize resource usage. Good enough is often good enough, but people must also know when perfection is really required (Seltzer 2013).

Agile and agility require that people know when good enough is really good enough. Once 80 percent of the user stories or requirements are delivered, then ask what is the real cost of attaining the final 20 percent? Do the benefits of perfection justify the costs?

Q27. What Is the Role of an Agile Coach?

A job description for an agile coach is loosely defined and evolving. An agile coach is experienced in executing agile projects and shares that experience with a team. The agile coach is responsible for providing feedback and advice to new agile project teams and to teams who want to perform at the highest level. The coach may be an outside expert, but he or she has worked in an agile environment and has often successfully run agile projects. An agile coach provides objective, unbiased guidance. An agile coach teaches team members to be agile and to follow an agile process. An agile coach helps an organization embrace agile as a culture shift.

Coaching is a process that aims to improve performance. A good coach helps a person realize their performance and potential. A coach strives to help a person learn and understand. A coach is a guide who inspires and empowers people. Coaching is a helping relationship. A great agile coach creates relationships and builds trust, asks questions and listens, and provides feedback and helps celebrate accomplishments. A coach strives to improve performance of those who are coached and increase satisfaction while improving the effectiveness of the team and meeting client and stakeholder goals.

Kelly (2009) noted that "reports from Yahoo! suggest that coaches can make a significant contribution. In this study, Scrum teams without coaching support increased their productivity by 35 percent, while those with coach support recorded 300 percent or greater improvement." He argues "Much of the coach's work is about changing individuals' mindsets, mental models, and shortcuts they have built up over years."

As explained in Chapter 2, a Scrum Master (SM) is a process coach rather than a project or team leader. A similar and sometimes complementary or overlapping role is a project lead or team lead. An agile team leader manages the project timeline, resources, and scope to meet business goals and requirements. On small teams, people in both roles take on other tasks to help complete a project. Each person is what is known in some sports as a utility player, a versatile person who can take on multiple roles competently and multitask.

According to White (2018), in a CIO article,

Agile coaches help train corporate teams on the agile methodology and oversee the development of agile teams to ensure effective outcomes for the organization. They are responsible for guiding teams through the implementation process and are tasked with encouraging workers and leadership to embrace the agile method.

She notes that the role of an SM is an entry-level role. Experience as an SM provides an agile coach real-world knowledge of the agile methodology and the intricacies of agile teams. Serving as an SM on an agile team gives a person a chance to encounter real-world issues and work with agile tools and software.

Depending upon past experiences, an agile coach may mentor executive teams, business analytics teams, consulting and IT development teams, or managers and employees in general. A coach is not a trainer, rather a coach is an experienced and trusted adviser and guide. A good coach offers support and assistance to those he or she is coaching to help them implement change and achieve desired goals.

An agile coach promotes understanding and adoption of agile principles and methods and is a catalyst for positive change in an organization.

Q28. How Do Experience and Self-Discipline Impact Agility?

Mental agility can be acquired, learned, and practiced. People can become more analytical and can think and understand more quickly in complex situations. Agility means a person or organization is quick and responsive in changing situations. Both experience and self-discipline positively impact agility of people and organizations.

Experience with agile means gaining practical knowledge and skill derived from direct observation, participation, and practice working in agile environments. Experience is the knowledge or mastery of a subject gained through direct involvement in or exposure to the practice of the subject. Empirical knowledge, the knowledge gained from doing and reflecting, is important because it creates deep knowledge based upon experience.

Self-discipline means to train yourself to do something by controlling your behavior and following processes and rules of behavior. Agile processes require disciplined behavior.

Mental agility is a term that describes people who are comfortable with complexity, have learned to examine problems carefully, can observe and make connections between different things and elements of a situation, and can explain the connections in a direct and straightforward way so others can understand. Organizational agility means managers in an organization have developed mental agility, have implemented agile processes, and managers anticipate environmental changes and are able and willing to implement needed organizational changes.

Q29. How Does an Agile Person Cope with Adversity?

People, teams, and organizations frequently encounter adverse or unfavorable circumstances, calamity, difficulties, or distress. Sometimes, adversity is an inevitable part of the change process; sometimes, it is extremely serious or continuous and must be overcome quickly. For example, it is common for teams and organizations trying agile for the first time to experience adversity like people resisting the change, miscommunications, status issues, project interruptions, and even conflict, cf., Pavkovic (2016). People with an agile mindset attack problems and tasks directly, work with a positive attitude, and provide suggestions to overcome adversity and obstacles. They care about their performance, the outcomes of their decision making, and about how decisions and performance impact their clients, team, and organization.

An agile person asks questions to understand what is in the best interests of the team, organization, and client. They strive to stay flexible and identify innovative solutions. An agile person experiments and gets feedback and uses that feedback to make continuous improvements in their actions and practices. A person with an agile mindset has a realistic and practical attitude that is focused on helping the team succeed. Howard (2015) argues that for a person with an agile mindset " 'There is no failure, only feedback.' It's about taking everything as lessons, adjusting actions according to the feedback, and proceeding toward desired outcomes, resulting in continuous improvement."

People often work together to cope with adversity and obstacles. People with diverse backgrounds are more likely to bring a fresh perspective when a team faces adversity or complexity. These resilient, diverse

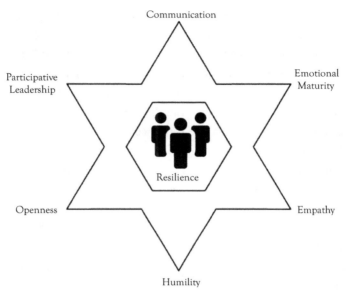

Communication

Participative
Leadership

Emotional
Maturity

Resilience

Openness

Empathy

Humility

Figure 6.1 Strengths of a diverse agile team

team members help the team and organization face the challenges. Kapp and Dame (2018) discuss strengths that agile teams can gain when diversity is embraced and sought. Figure 6.1 depicts the seven strengths of a diverse agile team include: (1) effective communication, (2) emotional maturity, (3) empathy, (4) humility, (5) openness, (6) resilience, and (7) participative leadership.

Overcoming adversity requires the right mindset—be positive and flexible. Agile people are courageous, accept change and responsibility, look for causes and solutions, communicate about existing or impending challenges, and do not make excuses. Feedback both positive and negative is sought and considered an opportunity to learn and grow. A person with an agile mindset stays focused on goals, opportunities, and strengths.

In general, an agile person copes with adversity by doing the following five activities:

1. *Monitoring what is occurring:* Let others know that you try to anticipate and avoid surprises. For people and teams moving from structured, bureaucratic approaches to an agile mindset, there are often many surprises that could not have been anticipated. Stay flexible,

adapt yourself to adverse circumstances, and *roll with the punches* as you take the agile journey.

2. *Seeking feedback and listening:* Positive and negative feedback both need to be considered and acted upon appropriately. Myatt (2012) recommends "talk less and listen more . . . The first rule in communication is to seek understanding before seeking to be understood. Communication is not a one-way street."

3. *Responding quickly and thoughtfully:* If a course of action does *not* appear to deliver results, admit that quickly, and then determine how to move on, how to change what you are doing. Agile people make mistakes too.

4. *Avoiding groupthink* (Janis 1971; Janis and Mann 1977; Cherry 2019): An agile person (1) should express opinions and creative thoughts, (2) should not self-censor, (3) should not coerce others and be the self-appointed censor, and (4) should not rush others to arrive at a forced consensus. In many cases, agility can be enhanced by seeking the advice of outsiders.

5. *Carefully making "one-way door" decisions:* Use facts and careful consideration when making decisions that involve a long-term commitment. Many agile actions can be reversed or even abandoned; they are two-way door decisions. Agile leaders strive to make high-quality, high-velocity decisions (Bezos 2015; Filloux 2017; Power and Heavin 2018). Making divisive decisions quickly and imposing them on others often leads to suboptimal and inappropriate decisions.

An agile person has accepted that ambiguity and various interpretations of facts exist, that the external world is increasingly volatile with high levels of uncertainty, that change is real and that problems must be overcome, that digital disruption is accelerating, and that situations are often complex and multicausal involving several causes and requiring careful analysis and critical thinking. An agile person tries to anticipate consequences and outcomes. Finally, an agile person adapts, avoids rationalizing, initiates change, responds to adversity, and removes barriers to success.

Becoming agile for a person, team, or organization is a challenging and never-ending journey, but it is worth it. There will be setbacks and adversity; agile is not solely a method; rather, it is a different way of thinking, understanding, and acting, cf., Denning 2018. Becoming agile and developing an agile mindset is a means of coping with adversity, enhancing customer value, and finding greater success.

Q30. What Are Common Barriers and Challenges to Becoming Agile?

We need to recognize that any major change is challenging. Becoming agile and doing agile is a major change! Managers who are transitioning to an agile mindset from a bureaucratic mindset will find the journey especially challenging. Organization culture and peoples' attitude are major barriers to becoming agile, cf., Krill (2013). Both attitude and behavioral changes are difficult; we know that people develop bad habits, and often, an organization's culture reinforces bad habits. A lack of experienced agile leaders is a barrier, but sometimes, that deficiency is more of an excuse.

Learning new ways to work can be viewed as burdensome, costly, and unnecessary. Some people are more comfortable with the routine of a bureaucratic process. These champions of details are more concerned with the procedure and reporting rather than on delivering value. In many organizations, following the rules that control activities become more important than delivering results. This reality hinders change.

The ideas of the Agile Manifesto are realistic, workable, and possible to implement. Latham (2019) argues that agile "is unworkable in practice for too many teams." We disagree. He argues most teams lack a foundation for calm, rational decision making. Perhaps that is true but training and culture can reinforce the need for calm and rationality. Supposedly, there is too much stress, anxiety, uncertainty, and pressure, so teams often abandon agile and do not reflect on outcomes, fail to prioritize, and neglect thinking about value. Agile teams must be insulated from stress, uncertainty, and other factors by senior managers. Working in short time-boxed periods with prioritized goals helps create greater certainty. People learn to cope with stress, pressure, uncertainty, and even anxiety. Contemporary organizations must develop cultures that support individuals and teams.

Most people have the intellectual capacity needed to become agile. Agile organizations and teams can benefit from including people with a wide range of abilities and interests. Becoming agile involves embracing and accepting change and learning to continually create change. Accepting that people have differential abilities and yet can contribute is part of becoming agile.

Agile is about much more than methods like Scrum, Extreme Programming (XP), and Feature Driven Development (FDD). Being agile means a team knows and uses selectively various methods and approaches. *But*, implementing agile is not some dogmatic, one-size-fits-all approach to change. Rather, agile gives people the freedom to try something new and to change and adapt while delivering value.

Denning (2012) identifies some attitude barriers to becoming agile. First, agile is perceived by some as a process that is only for star performers, and hence, most employees cannot become agile. This negative attitude is self-defeating. Second, some argue agile does not fit an organizational culture of respecting the chain of command and defining job responsibilities. Agile is not a chain of command way of working, but perhaps that approach no longer works in most situations. Third, some think agile methods only work for small projects. That is not true, multiple small agile teams can work together to deliver value on large projects. Fourth, agile can be effective without co-location. Face-to-face interactions among team members and stakeholders have benefits, but agile teams can be distributed geographically and successfully complete projects.

Also, according to Denning, there are process and structural obstacles. Agile is a mindset and it is not a *complete* methodology. Teams and managers often need to adopt additional project management processes. To find success, managers need to change and enhance the organization's reward system to motivate both individuals and teams. Agile is not limited or only appropriate for software development; an agile mindset can enhance and improve most projects.

An agile organization is an adhocracy and not a bureaucracy. An adhocracy is generally defined as a flexible, adaptable, and less formal organization. It uses specialized, multidisciplinary teams grouped by functions and projects. The organization has simple standardized procedures, limited rule-following, a shared division of responsibility, a flat hierarchy, and an emphasis on personal, collaborative relationships. Becoming an agile organization eliminates complicated rules and procedures.

Conclusion and Summary

Finding success means understanding how and when it is most effective to expend limited resources to maximize project outcomes. One heuristic guide to making decisions and allocating resources is the Pareto Principle. The principle states that roughly 80 percent of the output from a given situation or system is determined by 20 percent of the input. Pareto analysis helps managers prioritize and determine what has the greatest influence on overall goals.

An experienced agile coach can help achieve success. The coach is responsible for providing feedback and advice to new agile teams and to existing teams. The coach may be an internal or external expert, who has worked in an agile environment and has successfully completed agile projects. An agile coach mentors specific teams with a defined purpose, or managers and employees in general.

Today, organizations and people must respond quickly and appropriately to changing situations. Experience, agility, and self-discipline have a positive impact. Organizational agility means managers in an organization have developed mental agility, have implemented agile processes, and managers anticipate needed changes.

People should work together to cope with various impediments. People with diverse backgrounds are more likely to bring a fresh perspective when a team faces adversity or complexity. Resilient, diverse team members help the team and organization achieve goals. In general, overcoming adversity requires the right mindset; people should be positive and flexible.

Transitioning from a bureaucratic to an agile mindset is challenging. As we noted, people and culture are major barriers that hinder organizational transformation. There are challenges to becoming agile; these include perceptions of: (1) who can become agile, (2) the fit of agile with a highly structured chain of command, (3) the scope of projects for agile processes, and (4) that co-location is required for agile processes. These challenges can be overcome. To implement agile methods and processes in an organization, influential decision makers must want to become agile.

So, the quest for greater agility goes on and information technology is an increasing part of our lives.

Summary

Becoming Agile

Agile behaviors and processes are often better than rigid, bureaucratic ones. To succeed in the quest to become agile, *you* must think the quest is important and worthwhile. The journey will be challenging at times. The road is often long. "May the Road Rise Up to Meet You."

First, agile values and principles, when internalized, help to manage a volatile, uncertain, changing, and ambiguous situation. Agile values enhance the project development process and promote communication both horizontally and vertically throughout an organization. Also, agile practices enhance innovation through high-performance multidisciplinary teams and ensure business value by direct client involvement throughout the entire delivery process.

Second, agile does not prescribe a specific set of actions, behaviors, or steps. It is a culture, a worldview, and a mindset; it is not a methodology. In our view, agile is about learning to respond effectively to both the unexpected and the unplanned. Being agile is being people-focused, but successfully completing tasks is also important. More specifically, agile is about coordinated, incremental delivery. Agile is not about moving faster, rather it is about adaptability and learning. Also, agile processes should lead to more collaboration with stakeholders and better solutions.

Third, an agile mindset still requires the use of processes, tools, documentation, contract negotiation, and long- and short-range plans. It is important not to eliminate or neglect these activities and capabilities.

Fourth, an organization's transition from a plan-based approach to an agile approach should reduce management overhead and ease the burden of formalities for creative teams. Agile is about responding to and anticipating the customer and the market. Agile is about making the creation of value for customers the highest priority. When successfully applied to large projects and, potentially, an entire organization, agile can provide dramatic gains in effectiveness, efficiency, and value.

Fifth and finally, on our agile journey, we need to remember the advice of Thomas Edison that "there is no lasting failure, only feedback." Henry Ford noted *failure* is an opportunity to begin again. We must learn to approach everything as a lesson, learn to adjust our actions according to feedback, while proceeding toward desired outcomes. This approach results in continuous improvement. Agile mindset means you have joined the quest to continually learn.

Agility is now a key to business success. Fragile enterprises break, agile enterprises are more resilient. The importance of agility and developing an agile mindset has been increasing rapidly with a turbulent environment. An agile dance changes steps as the situation and the rhythm change. Do the agile dance that fits a situation and accept that change during the dance is OK. The dance may start as a slow waltz and change to the tango, then a line dance or quickstep . . . and then revert to a waltz or vice versa. There are few rules governing agile behavior and processes. Becoming agile is an ongoing journey that involves reflection, introspection, and thoughtfulness. One does not magically become agile; it is hard work. How far along are you and your organization on a journey to become agile?

Strive to think agile, do agile, and be agile. We hope you enjoy your journey.

Glossary

Agile: A mindset, a way of thinking, a framework for action taking, a goal, and a journey to more contingent processes, higher performance, and potentially greater value creation.

Agile Coach: Is a person responsible for providing feedback and advice to new agile project teams, and to teams who want to perform at the highest level.

Agile Development: Is an iterative approach to software delivery that builds software incrementally from the start of the project.

Agile Framework (also called an Agile Methodology): A framework that guides teams in an iterative and incremental delivery of a project goal and delivery of a defined *product*.

Agile Leader: Is a person with experience leading agile teams. They know what is important, and they must coach others in agile thinking and approaches.

Agile Organization: An organizing structure with decentralized decision making that is socially flat, team-oriented, and consensus-based. The five trademarks of an agile organization include: (1) a network of teams within (2) a people-centered culture that (3) operates in rapid learning and fast decision cycles, which are (4) enabled by technology, and a (5) common purpose that co-creates value for all stakeholders (Aghina, et al. 2018).

Agility: Is a firm's "ability to detect opportunities for innovation and seize those competitive market opportunities by assembling requisite assets, knowledge, and relationships with speed and surprise" (Sambamurthy, et al. 2003, p. 245).

Adaptive Planning: Is the ability to plan forward but altering the plan as circumstances change. It is an iterative process for organizing information flows, analyses, and special studies, facts, and opinions into decisions.

Agile Planning: Is one form of adaptive planning.

Agile Principle: Is a fundamental proposition that supports agile behavior and reasoning.

Agile Project Management (APM): Is an iterative, value-driven approach to delivering a project (Highsmith 2010).

Business Agility: Refers to the ability of managers of an organization to identify changes and challenges both internally and externally and to respond and adapt appropriately to deliver value to customers and meet stakeholder expectation, cf., www.agilealliance.org/glossary/business-agility

Extreme Programming (XP): Is an agile approach that aims to produce high-quality software and responsiveness to changing customer requirements by promoting simplicity in software development design, development, maintenance, and revision.

Feature-Driven Development (FDD): Is a client-centric, iterative, and incremental software development process focused on producing high-quality code through an intensive design, code, and inspection approach.

Kanban: Is about visualizing work, limiting work in progress, and maximizing efficiency.

Lean: Is an agile approach aimed at creating more value for customers using fewer resources.

Pareto Principle: Is a heuristic guide to making decisions and allocating resources. It states that approximately 80 percent of the output from a given situation or system is determined by 20 percent of the input.

Problem Framing: Involves explaining and describing the context of the problem in an understandable manner.

Product Backlog: Is a list of requirements or tasks for a system, expressed as a prioritized list of items.

Product Owner: Is a person who has final authority to represent the customer's interest in requirements prioritization as part of an agile project.

Project Portfolio Management (PPM): Is a coordination and control process that selects, prioritizes, and staffs programs and projects to align them with organizational strategies (Bridges 2018).

Project Vision Statement: An ideal view of desired outcomes for the client that result from successful project completion. A project vision statement is a vivid description of the project result intended to inspire the project stakeholders to initiate the project and to guide the project team. A project vision answers the *what* and *why* questions, and it provides a starting point for inspiring action.

Scrum: Is an agile framework and structured set of ideas that is intended to help teams collaborate on complex tasks.

Scrum Framework: Consists of scrum teams and their associated roles, events, artifacts, and rules.

Scrum Master: This role involves removing any impediments to progress, facilitating meetings, working with the team lead to make sure the task list or product backlog is in good shape and ready for the next short iteration or sprint.

Self-Organization: A management principle that teams autonomously organize their work. Self-organization happens within boundaries and in terms of given goals. Teams choose how best to accomplish their work, rather than receiving detailed direction from others outside the team.

Sprint: Is a short period of work during which an increment of product functionality is implemented.

Sprint Backlog: Defines the work for a sprint. It is the set of tasks that must be completed to realize the sprint's goal(s) and selected set of product backlog items.

Sprint Goal: Is the result of a negotiation between the product owner and the development team. Meaningful goals are specific and measurable.

Sprint Planning Meeting: Is a negotiation between the team and the product owner about what the team will do during the next sprint.

Sprint Retrospective Meeting: Is held at the end of every sprint after the sprint review meeting.

Stakeholder: Is any person external to an agile team with a specific interest in and knowledge of a product or project.

Stakeholder Engagement: Is a process used to involve people who may be affected by a decision so that they may influence the choice and implementation of the decision.

Team Lead or Project Lead: A person who works with the team and key stakeholders to set goals, schedules, and major objectives.

User Story: Is a high-level definition of a requirement, containing just enough information so that software developers can produce a reasonable estimate of the effort to implement it.

Value-Driven Delivery: Is the delivery of maximum business value in the minimum span of time. A team focuses on delivering the results defined in the Project Vision Statement and overcoming constraints of time, cost, scope, quality, people, and organizational capabilities to deliver value. Team members should understand what adds value to customers and users and then prioritize the high-value requirements.

Bibliography

Abtin, M. 2018. "The Agile Maturity Pyramid: What's the difference between Doing Agile and Being Agile?" *DXC.Technology Blog*, May 6, 2018, Available at https://blogs.dxc.technology/2018/05/06/the-agile-maturity-pyramid-whats-the-difference-between-doing-agile-and-being-agile/

Aghina, W., K. Ahlback, A. De Smet, G. Lackey, M. Lurie, M. Murarka, and C. Handscomb. 2018. "The Five Trademarks of Agile Organizations." *McKinsey Report*, January 2018, Available at https://mckinsey.com/business-functions/organization/our-insights/the-five-trademarks-of-agile-organizations

Almeida, I. 2018. "Scaling Agile is not the Path to Business Agility." *Medium*, June 16, 2018, Available at https://medium.com/nkd-collections/scaling-agile-is-not-the-path-to-business-agility-4ed1ed8465b6

Alterman, R. 1988. "Adaptive Planning." *Cognitive Science* 12, 393421, https://onlinelibrary.wiley.com/doi/pdf/10.1207/s15516709cog1203_3

AMA Dictionary, American Marketing Association, https://marketing-dictionary.org/a/adaptive-planning/

Ambler, S. 2012. "The Agile System Development Life Cycle (SDLC)." *Ambysoft*, Available at http://ambysoft.com/essays/agileLifecycle.html

Ambler, S. 2009. "Becoming Agile." Available at http://agiledata.org/essays/becomingAgile.html

Ambroziewicz, J. 2017. "Agile Will Kill Us All." *10clouds Blog*, May 12, 2017, Available at https://10clouds.com/blog/agile-kill/

Beck, K. 2001. "Manifesto for Agile Software Development." https://agilemanifesto.org/

Bezos, J. 2017. "20th Annual Letter to Amazon Shareholders." Available at https://sec.gov/Archives/edgar/data/1018724/000119312517120198/d373368dex991.htm

Bezos, J. 2015. "2015 Letter to Shareholders." *Amazon Annual Report*, January 30, 2015, Available at https://sec.gov/Archives/edgar/data/1018724/000119312516530910/d168744dex991.htm and Available at https://ir.aboutamazon.com/static-files/f124548c-5d0b-41a6-a670-d85bb191fcec

Bika, N. 2019. "The 14 Best Collaboration Tools for Productive Teams." *Workable*, Available at https://resources.workable.com/tutorial/collaboration-tools

Bradley, J., T. Lai, S. Meaney, S. Nguyen, and K. Brady. 2013. "Cisco Collaboration Work Practice Study." March, 2013, Available at https://cisco.com/c/dam/en/us/solutions/collaboration/collaboration-sales/cwps_full_report.pdf

Bridges, J. 2018. "5 Benefits in Adopting Project Portfolio Management." *Project Manager*, February 5, 2018, Available at https://projectmanager.com/training/5-benefits-adopting-project-portfolio-management

Brown, A.W. 2013. *Enterprise Software Delivery: Bringing Agility and Efficiency to the Global Software Supply Chain*. Upper Saddle River, NJ: Addison-Wesley.

Chaos Report. 2011. "Agile Succeeds Three Times More Often Than Waterfall." Available at http://mountaingoatsoftware.com/blog/agile-succeeds-three-times-more-often-than-waterfall

Cherry, K. 2019. "How to Recognize and Avoid Groupthink." *Verywellmind*, September 26, at URL https://verywellmind.com/what-is-group think-2795213

Cockburn, A. 2001. "Agile Software Development." *Addison-Wesley Professional*, October 22, ISBN-10: 0201699699

Cohn, M. 2004. *User Stories Applied: For Agile Software Development*.

Conrad, A. 2018. "What Exactly Is Agile? A Definition of Agile Project Management." *Capterra*, November 18, 2018, Available at https://blog.capterra.com/definition-of-agile-project-management/Ali

Dam, R. 2019. "The Pareto Principle and How to Be More Effective." October 2019, Available at https://interaction-design.org/literature/article/the-pareto-principle-and-how-to-be-more-effective

Denning, S. 2012. "The Case Against Agile: Ten Perennial Management Objections." *Forbes*, April 17, 2012, Available at https://forbes.com/sites/stevedenning/2012/04/17/the-case-against-agile-ten-perennial-management-objections/#2147c493a955

Denning, S. 2018. "The 12 Stages Of The Agile Transformation Journey." *Forbes*, November 4, 2018, Available at https://forbes.com/sites/steve denning/2018/11/04/the-twelve-stages-of-the-agile-transformation-journey/#47cd06df3dd4

Drucker, P.F. 1954. *The Practice of Management*. New York, NY: Harper & Row.

Eljay-Adobe. 2017. "Scrum is Easy." *DEV*, September 12, 2017, updated on February 06, 2018, Available at https://dev.to/eljayadobe/scrum-is-easy.

Filloux, F. 2017. "Lessons from the 'Bezos Way' and the Success of Amazon." *Quartz*, April 18, 2017, Available at https://qz.com/961350/lessons-from-the-bezos-way-and-the-success-of-amazon/

Fried, J., and D.H. Hansson. 2010. *Rework*. Vermilion, UK.

Fowler, M. 2014. "ShuHaRi." August 22, 2014, https://martinfowler.com/bliki/ShuHaRi.html

Frick, T. 2016. "Five lessons learned from Agile Processes." *Mightybytes Blog, Business Strategy, Events and Workshops*, Available at https://mightybytes.com/blog/five-lessons-learned-from-agile-processes/

Getzels, J.W., and M. Csikszentmihalyi. 1976. "The creative Vision: A Longitudinal Study of Problem Finding in Art." *Creative Education* 4, no. 9, September 6, 2013, New York, NY: John Wiley & Sons, Available at https://scirp.org/(S(i43dyn45teexjx455qlt3d2q))/reference/ReferencesPapers.aspx?ReferenceID=932873

Hagar, M. 2019. "Right to Left." October 12, 2020, Avaialable at https://agileontheedge.com/2019/08/14/mike-burrows-right-to-left/

Hansen, B. 2016. "7 Ways to Improve Team Performance." *Wrike Blog*, November 15, 2016, Available at https://wrike.com/blog/7-ways-improve-team-performance

Harris, T. 2010. "Internal and External Influences on Performance." *Octane Blog*, December 30, 2010, Avaialble at https://blog.eonetwork.org/2010/12/1829/

Highsmith, J. 2010. *Agile Project Management: Creating Innovative Products*, 2nd ed. Addison-Wesley Professional.

Highsmith, J. 2004. *Agile Project Management: Creating Innovative Products*. Addison-Wesley Professional.

Howard, L. 2015. "What Does It Mean to Have an Agile Mindset?" *AgileConnection*, April 1, 2015, Available at https://agileconnection.com/article/what-does-it-mean-have-agile-mindset

Janis, I.L. 1971. "Groupthink." *Psychology Today* 5, no. 6, pp. 43–46, 74–76.

Janis, I.L., and L. Mann. 1977. *Decision Making: A Psychological Analysis of Conflict, Choice, and Commitment*. New York, NY: Free Press.

Kapp, U., and D. Dame. 2018. "7 Strengths of Highly Diverse Agile Teams." October 8, 2020, Available at https://scrum.org/resources/7-strengths-highly-diverse-agile-teams

Kelly, A. 2009. "The Role of the Agile Coach." *Agile Connection*, November 3, 2009, Available at https://agileconnection.com/article/role-agile-coach

Kruse, K. 2016. "The 80/20 Rule and How It Can Change Your Life." *Forbes*, March 07, 2016, Available at https://forbes.com/sites/kevinkruse/2016/03/07/80-20-rule/#5b6319e23814

Latham, H. 2019. "A Critique of Agile theory—and Why Agile Rarely Works in Practice." *UX Collective*, May 13, 2019, Available at https://uxdesign.cc/a-critique-of-agile-theory-f60fa7c28900

Mandir, E. 2018. "Going Agile? The Excitement Won't Last." *Medium.com*, January 24, 2018, Available at https://medium.com/inside-agile/going-agile-the-excitement-wont-last-7ce01ce326de

McGannon, B. 2013. "Agile Project Management Foundations." Lynda.com

McKinsey & Company. 2020. "Enterprise Agility—Your Last ever Reorganization." October 25, 2020, Available at https://mckinsey.com/business-functions/organization/how.../enterprise-agility

Mersino, A. 2018. "Agile Leader Role during an Agile Transformation." *Vitality Chicago*, November 30, 2018, Available at https://vitalitychicago.com/blog/what-leaders-role-agile-transformation/

Meyer, P. 2015. *The Agility Shift: Creating Agile and Effective Leaders, Teams, and Organizations*. Taylor & Francis.

Mitchell, R., B. Agle, and D. Wood. 1997. "Toward a Theory of Stakeholder Identification and Salience: Defining the Principle of Who and What Really Counts." *Academy of Management Review* 22, no. 4, pp. 853–858.

Mitchell, I. 2019. "Becoming Agile: Evidence Based Management." *Scrum.org*, March 8, 2019, Available at https://scrum.org/resources/blog/becoming-agile-evidence-based-management

Mullaiselvan, M. 2009. "The Pareto Principle/80-20 rule/the Law of the Vital Few and the Principle of Factor Sparsity." *Blog Post,* May 09, 2009, Available at https://sites.google.com/site/mullais/Home/misc/the-pareto-principle-80-20-rule-the-law-of-the-vital-few-and-the-principle-of-factor-sparsity

Myatt, M. 2012. "Why Most Leaders Need to Shut Up and Listen." *Forbes*, February 9, 2012, Available at https://forbes.com/sites/mikemyatt/2012/02/09/why-most-leaders-need-to-shut-up-listen/#4b696acb6ef9

Nicolaas, D. 2018. *Scrum for Teams: A Guide by Practical Example*. Business Expert Press.

Nieuwland, J. 2018. "28 Best Collaboration Tools To Improve Teamwork in 2018." *Workzone*, June 1, 2017, Available at https://workzone.com/blog/collaboration-tools/

Oswald, M. 2016. "What is Value-Driven Delivery in the Agile World?" *Whizlabs*, August 12, 2016, Available at https://whizlabs.com/blog/what-is-value-driven-delivery-in-the-agile-world/

Paquette, P., and M. Frankl. 2015. *Agile Project Management for Business Transformation Success*. Business Expert Press.

Pavkovic, L. 2016. "6 Challenges in Applying Scrum and How to Overcome Them." *DZone*, September 29, Available at https://dzone.com/articles/6-challenges-in-applying-scrum-and-how-to-overcome

Parziale, J. 2017. "5 Phases of an Agile Project Management Framework." *LinkedIn*, August 15, 2017, Available at https://linkedin.com/pulse/5-phases-agile-project-management-framework-jonathan-parziale-csm

Pentland, A. 2012. "The New Science of Building Great Teams." *Harvard Business Review*, April, Available at https://hbr.org/2012/04/the-new-science-of-building-great-teams

Peppers, D. 2018. "Why 'You Can't Manage What You Can't Measure' is Bad Advice." *LinkedIn*, August 31, 2018, Available at https://linkedin.com/pulse/why-you-cant-manage-what-measure-bad-advice-don-peppers/

Power, D.J., and C. Heavin. 2018. *Data-Based Decision Making and Digital Transformation*. Business Expert Press.

Rigby, D.K., J. Sutherland. and H. Takeuchi. 2016. "Embracing Agile." *Harvard Business Review*, May 2016, Available at https://hbr.org/2016/05/embracing-agile

Ronan, B. 2016. "10 Reasons You Should be Using Agile." *CIO*, June 6, 2016, Available at, https://cio.com/article/3078178/10-reasons-you-should-be-using-agile.html

Rubin, K.S. 2013. *Essential Scrum: A Practical Guide to the Most Popular Agile Process*. Boston: Addison-Wesley.

Sambamurthy, V., A. Bharadwaj, and V. Grover. 2003. "Shaping Agility through Digital Options: Reconceptualizing the Role of Information Technology in Contemporary Firms." *MIS Quarterly* 27, no. 2, pp. 237–263.

Sanchez, F., E. Bonjour, J. Micaëlli, and D. Monticolo. May-August, 2019. "A Step for Improving the Transition Between Traditional Project Management to Agile Project Management Using a Project Management Maturity Model." *Journal of Modern Project Management* 7, no. 1, pp. 102–119, Available at https://journalmodernpm.com/index.php/jmpm/article/view/455

Schmitz, K. Spring, 2018. "A Three Cohort Study of Role-Play Instruction for Agile Project Management." *Journal of Information Systems Education*, 29, no. 2, pp. 93–103, Available at https://aisel.aisnet.org/jise/vol29/iss2/5/

Schwaber, K., and J. Sutherland. 2017. "The Official Scrum Guide." *Scrumguides.org*, November 2017, Available at https://scrumguides.org/download.html

Schwaber, K. 2004. Agile Project Management with Scrum, Microsoft Press.

Seltzer, L.F. 2013. "How Do You Know What's Good Enough?" *Psychology Today*, October 16, 2013, Available at https://psychologytoday.com/us/blog/evolution-the-self/201310/how-do-you-know-whats-good-enough

Sliger, M. 2009. "Agile Ethics and Values." *AgileConnection*, January 28, 2009, Available at https://agileconnection.com/article/agile-ethics-and-values

Smith, G. 2012. "What Does it take to Become Agile?" Paper presented at PMI® Global Congress 2012—North America, Vancouver, British Columbia, Canada. Newtown Square, PA: Project Management Institute, Available at https://pmi.org/learning/library/take-become-agile-5971

Todaro, D. 2020. "9 Lessons Learned from Experts Practicing Agile." *Ascendle*, January 17, 2020, Available at https://ascendle.com/insight/blog/9-lessons-learned-from-experts-practicing-agile/

Usmani, F. 2012. "Stakeholder Management Strategy in Project Management." *PM Study Circle*, December 13, 2019, Available at https://pmstudycircle.com/2012/06/stakeholder-analysis-stakeholder-management-strategy/

Wake, W. 2003. "INVEST in Good Stories, and SMART Tasks." Available at https://xp123.com/articles/invest-in-good-stories-and-smart-tasks/

White, S.K. 2008. "What is an Agile Coach? A Valuable Role for Organizational Change." *CIO*, August 8, 2018, Available at https://cio.com/article/3294700/agile-coach-role-defined.html

About the Authors

Daniel J. Power is a Professor of Information Systems and Management at the College of Business Administration at the University of Northern Iowa, Cedar Falls, Iowa, USA. He is also the editor of DSSResources. com. His primary research streams examine computerized decision support and digital transformation of organizational decision-making behavior. Power has published more than 50 refereed journal articles and book chapters, more than 30 refereed proceedings papers, and seven books. His expanded DSS Framework has received widespread interest. Dr. Power's 2018 book with Ciara Heavin is titled *Data-based Decision Making and Digital Transformation*.

Ciara Heavin is a Professor in Business Information Systems at Cork University Business School, University College Cork, Ireland. Her research focuses on opportunities for using information systems (IS) in the global health care ecosystem and in digital transformation. Ciara has directed funded research in the investigation, development, and implementation of innovative technology solutions in the health care domain. She has published articles in several top international IS journals and conference proceedings. This is the third book Ciara has coauthored with Daniel J. Power: *Decision Support, Analytics, and Business Intelligence*; *Data-Based Decision Making and Digital Transformation*; and now *On Becoming Agile*.

Index

OTHER TITLES IN THE
INFORMATION SYSTEMS COLLECTION

Daniel Power, University of Northern Iowa, Editor

- *Computers and Information Processing for Business* by Sergio Ribeiro
- *Mastering the 7 Dimensions of Business-Technology Alignment* by Ashish Pachory
- *Aligning Technology with Business for Digital Transformation* by Ashish Pachory
- *Creating a Culture for Information Systems Success, Second Edition* by Zakariya Belkhamza
- *Business Continuity in a Cyber World* by David Sutton
- *Data-Based Decision Making and Digital Transformation* by Daniel J. Power and Ciara Heavin
- *Computer Support for Successful Project Management* by Ulhas Samant
- *Successful ERP Systems* by Jack G. Nestell and David L. Olson
- *Decision Support, Analytics, and Business Intelligence, Third Edition* by Daniel J. Power and Ciara Heavin
- *Building Successful Information Systems* by Michael Savoie
- *Computer Support for Successful Project Management* by Ulhas Samant
- *Information Technology Security Fundamentals* by Glen Sagers and Bryan Hosack
- *Creating a Culture for Information Systems Success* by Zakariya Belkhamza
- *Decision Support, Analytics, and Business Intelligence* by Daniel Power
- *Building Successful Information Systems* by Michael Savoie

Announcing the Business Expert Press Digital Library

Concise e-books business students need for classroom and research

This book can also be purchased in an e-book collection by your library as

- a one-time purchase,
- that is owned forever,
- allows for simultaneous readers,
- has no restrictions on printing, and
- can be downloaded as PDFs from within the library community.

Our digital library collections are a great solution to beat the rising cost of textbooks. E-books can be loaded into their course management systems or onto students' e-book readers.
The **Business Expert Press** digital libraries are very affordable, with no obligation to buy in future years. For more information, please visit **www.businessexpertpress.com/librarians**. To set up a trial in the United States, please email **sales@businessexpertpress.com**.

CPSIA information can be obtained
at www.ICGtesting.com
Printed in the USA
LVHW021626011222
734350LV00003B/488

9 781637 420089